S. Hrg. 113–50

THE FUTURE OF DRONES IN AMERICA: LAW ENFORCEMENT AND PRIVACY CONSIDERATIONS

HEARING

BEFORE THE

COMMITTEE ON THE JUDICIARY UNITED STATES SENATE

ONE HUNDRED THIRTEENTH CONGRESS

FIRST SESSION

MARCH 20, 2013

Serial No. J–113–10

Printed for the use of the Committee on the Judiciary

U.S. GOVERNMENT PRINTING OFFICE

81–775 PDF WASHINGTON : 2013

For sale by the Superintendent of Documents, U.S. Government Printing Office
Internet: bookstore.gpo.gov   Phone: toll free (866) 512–1800; DC area (202) 512–1800
Fax: (202) 512–2104   Mail: Stop IDCC, Washington, DC 20402–0001

COMMITTEE ON THE JUDICIARY

PATRICK J. LEAHY, Vermont, *Chairman*

DIANNE FEINSTEIN, California	CHUCK GRASSLEY, Iowa, *Ranking Member*
CHUCK SCHUMER, New York	ORRIN G. HATCH, Utah
DICK DURBIN, Illinois	JEFF SESSIONS, Alabama
SHELDON WHITEHOUSE, Rhode Island	LINDSEY GRAHAM, South Carolina
AMY KLOBUCHAR, Minnesota	JOHN CORNYN, Texas
AL FRANKEN, Minnesota	MICHAEL S. LEE, Utah
CHRISTOPHER A. COONS, Delaware	TED CRUZ, Texas
RICHARD BLUMENTHAL, Connecticut	JEFF FLAKE, Arizona
MAZIE HIRONO, Hawaii	

BRUCE A. COHEN, *Chief Counsel and Staff Director*
KOLAN DAVIS, *Republican Chief Staff Director*

CONTENTS

STATEMENTS OF COMMITTEE MEMBERS

Page

Cornyn, Hon. John, a U.S. Senator from the State of Texas, prepared statement 69
Grassley, Hon. Chuck, a U.S. Senator from the State of Iowa 3
Leahy, Hon. Patrick J., a U.S. Senator from the State of Vermont 1
    prepared statement 73

WITNESSES

Calo, Ryan, Assistant Professor, University of Washington School of Law, Seattle, Washington 10
Miller, Benjamin, Unmanned Aircraft Program Manager, Mesa County Sheriff's Office, Mesa County, Colorado, and Representative, Airborne Law Enforcement Association 5
Stepanovich, Amie, Director, Domestic Surveillance Project, Electronic Privacy Information Center, Washington, DC 7
Toscano, Michael, President and Chief Executive Officer, Association for Unmanned Vehicle Systems International, Arlington, Virginia 8

QUESTIONS AND ANSWERS

Responses of Ryan Calo to questions submitted by Senators Grassley and Lee 33
Responses of Benjamin Miller to questions submitted by Senators Grassley and Lee 39
Responses of Amie Stepanovich to questions submitted by Senator Grassley ... 42
Responses of Michael Toscano to questions submitted by Senators Grassley and Lee 48

SUBMISSIONS FOR THE RECORD

American Civil Liberties Union (ACLU), Laura W. Murphy, Director, Washington, DC, statement 58
Calo, Ryan, Assistant Professor, University of Washington School of Law, Seattle, Washington, statement 70
Miller, Benjamin, Unmanned Aircraft Program Manager, Mesa County Sheriff's Office, Mesa County, Colorado, and Representative, Airborne Law Enforcement Association, statement 75
Stepanovich, Amie, Director, Domestic Surveillance Project, Electronic Privacy Information Center (epic.org), Washington, DC, statement 84
Toscano, Michael, President and Chief Executive Officer, Association for Unmanned Vehicle Systems International (AUVSI), Arlington, Virginia: statement 92
    (AUVSI), attachments 97

ADDITIONAL SUBMISSIONS FOR THE RECORD

Submissions for the record not printed due to voluminous nature, previously printed by an agency of the Federal Government or other criteria determined by the Committee, list:
    The Economic Impact of Unmanned Aircraft Systems Integration in the United States, AUVSI, Report, March 2013

THE FUTURE OF DRONES IN AMERICA: LAW ENFORCEMENT AND PRIVACY CONSIDERATIONS

WEDNESDAY, MARCH 20, 2013

U.S. SENATE,
COMMITTEE ON THE JUDICIARY,
Washington, D.C.

The Committee met, pursuant to notice, at 10:38 a.m., in room SD–226, Dirksen Senate Office Building, Hon. Patrick J. Leahy, Chairman of the Committee, presiding.

Present: Senators Leahy, Feinstein, Durbin, Klobuchar, Franken, Blumenthal, Hirono, Grassley, Lee, and Cruz.

OPENING STATEMENT OF HON. PATRICK J. LEAHY, A U.S. SENATOR FROM THE STATE OF VERMONT

Chairman LEAHY. I appreciate everybody being here, and as you know, we are having budget and other matters going on. That is why some of us are in and out of this hearing.

I had breakfast this morning with the Chairman of the Joint Chiefs of Staff, General Dempsey. When I mentioned this hearing, I pointed out to him that this is on domestic, non-military use of drones. Recently the debate about the use of unmanned aerial vehicles, or ''drones,'' has largely focused on the lethal targeting of suspected terrorists, including Americans. I continue to have deep concerns about the constitutional and legal implications of such targeted killings, and both Senator Grassley and I have requested all the OLC material on that. I have spoken with Senator Durbin, who next month will chair a hearing in the Constitution Subcommittee that is going to examine these issues carefully.

As I noted at the beginning of this Congress, I am convinced that the domestic use of drones to conduct surveillance and collect other information will have a broad and significant impact on the everyday lives of millions of Americans. Just in the last decade, technological advancements have revolutionized aviation to make this technology cheaper and more readily available. As a result, many law enforcement agencies, private companies, and individuals have expressed interest in operating drones in our national airspace. I should mention that we are not talking just about the large Predator drones that are being used by the military or along our borders, but also about smaller, lightweight unmanned vehicles. We are going to hear testimony about that. The one that Mr. Sheehan is bringing up here now is from the Mesa County Sheriff's Office, and if you could just hold that up there. That weighs just 2 or 3 pound—2 pounds. Thank you, Mr. Miller. That weighs 2 pounds.

With the Federal Aviation Administration estimating that as many as 30,000 drones like this will be operating in the national airspace by the end of this decade, I think we have to carefully consider the policy implications of this fast-emerging technology.

I know that we are going to hear a lot of things about the unique advantages of using unmanned aircraft as opposed to manned vehicles. Drones are able to carry out arduous and dangerous tasks that would otherwise be expensive or difficult for a human to undertake. For example, in addition to law enforcement surveillance, drones will potentially be used for scientific experiments, agricultural research, geological surveying, pipeline maintenance, and search-and-rescue operations.

So there are many valuable uses, but at the same time, the use of unmanned aircraft raises serious concerns about the impact on the constitutional and privacy rights of all Americans. The Department of Homeland Security, through Customs and Border Protection, already operates modified, unarmed drones to patrol rural parts of our northern and southern borders, as well as to support drug interdiction efforts by law enforcement. A number of local law enforcement agencies have begun to explore using drones to assist with operational surveillance. This raises a number of questions regarding the adequacy of current privacy laws and the scope of existing Fourth Amendment jurisprudence. When is it appropriate for law enforcement to use a drone, and for what purposes? Under what circumstances should law enforcement be required to first obtain a search warrant? And then what should be done with the data that is collected and how long should it be kept? And although no drones operating in the U.S. are yet weaponized, I am advised, should law enforcement be permitted to equip unmanned aircraft with non-lethal tools such as tear gas or pepper spray?

My concerns about the domestic use of drones extend beyond Government and law enforcement. Before we allow widespread use of drones in the domestic airspace, we have to carefully consider the impact on the privacy rights of Americans. Just last week, we were reminded how one company's push to gather data on Americans led vast over-collection and potential privacy violations.

Similarly, a simple scan of amateur videos on the Internet demonstrates how prevalent drone technology is becoming among private citizens. Small, quiet unmanned aircraft can easily be built or purchased online for only a few hundred dollars and then equipped with high-definition video cameras while flying in areas impossible for manned aircraft to operate without being detected. It is not hard to imagine the serious privacy problems that this type of technology could cause. In a State like mine, in Vermont, where we protect and guard our privacy, this is raising some very serious questions from people from the far right to the far left.

So we cannot take a short-sighted view. Technology in this area will advance at an incredible rate. So I hope this hearing will be just the beginning of a dialogue.

To help this Committee explore some of these issues, Senator Grassley and I have invited witnesses who will testify from a variety of perspectives. We will hear from a law enforcement official who has a functioning and fully operational unmanned aircraft unit; we will hear from the head of the leading unmanned vehicle industry group; a representative from the Electronic Privacy Information Center; and a scholar who has studied the intersection of drone technology with privacy and Fourth Amendment law. And I appreciate them being here.

Senator Grassley.

STATEMENT OF HON. CHUCK GRASSLEY, A U.S. SENATOR FROM THE STATE OF IOWA

Senator GRASSLEY. Before I go to my statement, listening to you I believe I can summarize by saying I do not believe there is any differences between your concern and my concern on this issue. So I am glad to have that working relationship on this issue.

As we examine drone technologies, we continue our efforts to properly balance innovation, privacy, and public safety. There are tremendous benefits to society from drone technology. The technology can help first responders quickly identify the nature and scope of, example, a forest fire or natural disaster. It may help police respond more quickly in cases involving hostage rescue, missing children, or a child abduction. With drones carrying advanced technology that provide facial recognition, license plate recognition, biometric recognition, important investigative leads can be pursued rapidly.

An area where drones may be of particular use is in helping secure our vast borders. The drone technology is now becoming part of a larger border security strategy. Drone technology can help increase our security on the borders while reducing the costs to our taxpayers.

The Government has a heightened interest in protecting the borders, and the Constitution allows greater use of surveillance at points of entry, so I plan to continue discussions with Homeland Security about their use of this *technology to make sure that we are maximizing it.

On the surveillance side, many questions about drone technology remain. Drones can go almost anywhere and can maintain surveillance, sometimes with some equipment for days. They carry sophisticated technology, greatly enhancing surveillance. The potential benefit to drone technology is limited only by the imagination, but we must always remember that the power of new technology creates greater responsibility to respect the privacy of our citizens.

While drones can expand the reach of a criminal investigation, they can also create an increased risk of invading privacy. We need to make sure that we have sufficient legal safeguards in place to promote innovation while balancing public safety and the privacy of law-abiding citizens. We should carefully consider what Government can constitutionally do.

But as a matter of policy, we should go further and we should examine what limitations are appropriate to protect our privacy. Just because the Government may comply with the Constitution does not mean that they should be allowed to constantly surveil like Big Brother.

The thought of Government drones buzzing overhead monitoring the activities of law-abiding citizens runs contrary to the notion of what it means to live in a free society. The Fourth Amendment prohibition on unreasonable searches and seizures has a consistent meaning, but the tests for determining whether Fourth Amendment rights have been violated have changed as technology changes. For more than 40 years, a physical trespass was necessary. For more than 40 years after that, the inquiry has been whether an individual's reasonable expectation of privacy has been violated.

The recent Supreme Court case of *U.S.* v. *Jones* examined whether advanced technology is so intrusive that it becomes a trespass, in violation of the Fourth Amendment. That case is a good starting point for a discussion on drones.

Example: Innovations in communication technology such as mobile devices have exposed formerly private information to public scrutiny. Information once closely guarded is now easily accessible via the Internet on simply handheld mobile devices. These developments and the ability of drones to provide unprecedented surveillance may lead to new standards establishing Fourth Amendment violations.

The use of drones for law enforcement also raises a new challenge for prosecutors. Both the Chairman and I have at times referred to the famous speech Robert Jackson delivered when he was Attorney General. In that speech, Jackson pointed out that it is possible to find at least a technical violation of criminal law on the part of almost anyone. Good prosecutors will use these powerful new surveillance tools wisely. However, not all prosecutors are as responsible as we expect them to be, and our oversight responsibilities will be even more important as technology evolves.

I have already started asking questions. Example: Last June, when the Attorney General appeared before the Committee, I asked him whether the Department was using or planning to use drones for law enforcement purposes. To date, I have not received an answer. This, even after another appearance before us this month. It is very important that the American people know whether and how the Justice Department is going to use these machines.

Failure to provide answers about the use of these technologies is very concerning as well. It may well be subject for further legislation. That is something that the Chairman and I obviously will discuss. That is why today's hearing is so important, to answer questions, and not all of these questions can I give you because I do not have time. But whether we draw the limit regarding the use of drones by Government agencies—where do we draw that line? Under what circumstances do we require a search warrant? Should police use drones only for surveillance? Should local governments be allowed to use drones to search for traffic violations and building code violations? Should the Federal Government use drones to follow around disability claimants to see whether they are fraudulent? What reasonable limitations are appropriate for where and when to use drones?

Additionally, in examining the use of drones by the Government, Congress also needs to examine the reasonable use and limits of drones by private citizens in the private sector. Where do we draw the line in balancing the media's rights under the First Amendment with citizens' rights to be protected from invasion of privacy?

Another area to examine is innovative use of drones, and so coming from a rural State, as the Chairman does, we have a lot of agriculture. Drones can be used by farmers to provide a bird's-eye view of a field and help a farmer survey crops more quickly for early signs of pests or disease. Drones may be able to spray crops to maintain their vigor, check livestock, prevent of crop, livestock, and equipment. These are all time-saving and cost-saving benefits to agriculture. But no farmer would appreciate Government drones constantly flying overhead playing the role of Big Brother. And no one wants drone technology to end up in the hands of a harassing neighbor, child predator, stalker, drug dealer, violent criminal, or terrorist.

These are challenges we face in our effort to properly balance innovation, privacy, and public safety, and this is a very appropriate hearing for this Committee to have.

Thank you, Mr. Chairman, for your leadership.

Chairman LEAHY. Thank you very much.

Our first witness is Ben Miller, who has probably been listening to what we are saying here and wondering just where this might lead. He is a 13-year veteran of the Mesa County Sheriff's Office in Colorado. He is also the Unmanned Aircraft Program manager for the Mesa County Sheriff's Office, a designation you would not have seen in many sheriff's offices just a decade ago. He is a representative of the Airborne Law Enforcement Association. He has assisted the Federal Aviation Administration with developing regulations regarding the public use of unmanned aircraft systems.

What I am going to do is put all statements in the record as though read in full, but if you would like to summarize, please, Mr. Miller, we would appreciate it. Is your microphone—there you go.

Mr. MILLER. There we go. Is that on?

Chairman LEAHY. Yes.

STATEMENT OF BENJAMIN MILLER, UNMANNED AIRCRAFT PROGRAM MANAGER, MESA COUNTY SHERIFF'S OFFICE, MESA COUNTY, COLORADO, AND REPRESENTATIVE, AIRBORNE LAW ENFORCEMENT ASSOCIATION

Mr. MILLER. Well, good morning, Chairman Leahy and members of the Committee. My name is Benjamin Miller. I am the Unmanned Aircraft Program manager with the Mesa County Sheriff's Office and, as said, a representative of the Airborne Law Enforcement Association.

Thank you for inviting me to speak to you about the use of unmanned aircraft in the small Colorado community where I live. The Mesa County Sheriff's Office is a middle-sized agency of 200 people with a patrol team of just over 65 deputies. These deputies serve approximately 175,000 citizens who live inside a 3,300-square-mile county. We see a wide range of criminal activity, from petty offenses to major crimes, including drug trafficking and homicide.

In 4 years, we have flown more operational hours than anyone else in the country, with 185 hours in just over 40 missions, with two small, battery-operated unmanned aircraft systems. That is a lot considering the Draganflyer X6, which is this one on the table here, is a backpack-sized helicopter that can fly for only 15 minutes and weighs 2 pounds. Our small airplane, called Falcon UAV, can fly for an hour and can fit in the trunk of a car and weighs just 8 pounds. Both systems are used to carry cameras, which are commercially available. In fact, you can buy the very same camera that we put on the Draganflyer X6 at Walmart.

I would like to share with you today some brief examples of how we have used this equipment.

My first example occurred last May when an historic church caught fire. We flew the Draganflyer X6, carrying a thermal camera, which allowed us to show the hot spots that still needed to be properly extinguished. Firemen were then able to assess the situation and address it accordingly, as these areas were not viewable to the naked eye. We flew about 60 feet in the air and took photos that the arson investigators were able to use to determine which direction the fire had traveled through the building.

My next example occurred just a few weeks ago when a 62-year-old woman went missing. We launched our Falcon UAV in an effort to find this woman. We were able to clear large areas in a short time that would normally take much longer and involve more resources and cost a lot more money. The woman's body was recovered by ground personnel the following day. The use of Falcon allowed us to more directly apply our resources in this recovery effort.

My final example occurred just days ago. It really does not have a whole lot to do with law enforcement, but it does offer a glimpse into the real benefit of unmanned aerial systems and, that is, affordability. Each year, Mesa County spends nearly $10,000 on a manned aerial survey of our landfill to determine the increase in waste over the previous year. My team and I completed that very same survey for a mere $200. By flying back and forth over the landfill, we were able to combine the photos that we took with geographic reference data and provide a volume to the landfill to an accuracy of 10 cubic centimeters.

While military unmanned aircraft fly for hours and sometimes days at enormous altitudes, we fly just minutes to photograph a crime scene and cannot exceed an hour of flight time. The FAA has strict protocols that only allow us to fly during the day, and we cannot fly more than 400 feet off the ground.

While military unmanned aircraft are both large in size and cost, our equipment is small and relatively inexpensive. Our equipment does not possess the capability to carry sensors that can read license plates from space or look through your home or carry weapons.

Just recently, I was on the Airborne Law Enforcement Association's website and found a 1934 photo of an airborne police officer in a gyrocopter with a telegraph machine strapped to his leg. Aviation and public safety have a longstanding relationship. While unmanned aircraft cannot recover a stranded motorist in a swollen river, they can provide an aerial view for a fraction of the cost of manned aviation. I estimate unmanned aircraft can complete 30 percent of the missions of manned aviation for 2 percent of the cost. The Mesa County Sheriff's Office projects direct cost of unmanned flight at just $25 an hour as compared to the cost of manned aviation that can range from $250 to thousands of dollars an hour. It actually costs just one cent to charge the flight battery that we use inside our system.

My agency's use of unmanned aircraft is primarily for search and rescue and crime scene reconstruction, but it must be said that any tool can be abused. This sad reality is not unique to law enforcement, nor did it begin with unmanned aircraft. While the use of unmanned aircraft requires specific policies and procedures, the handling of sensitive photographs and video has been around law enforcement for years. And I can speak to a strong code of conduct policy inside my own agency that addresses more than just the use of unmanned aircraft. Leadership organizations like the International Association of Chiefs of Police have recently released unmanned aircraft policy guidelines that encourage agencies to adopt non-retention policies, whereby the information that we collect that is not determined evidence is deleted. These guidelines have also been endorsed by the Airborne Law Enforcement Association, and it is with their guidance that agencies like mine are developing robust policies, quality training tools, and professional unmanned aircraft programs.

In closing, I hope that my testimony has offered a realistic perspective of the many benefits of unmanned aircraft. Thank you for the opportunity.

[The prepared statement of Mr. Miller appears as a submission for the record.]

Chairman LEAHY. Thank you very much.

Our next witness, Amie Stepanovich, is the Director of the Electronic Privacy Information Center's Domestic Surveillance Program. Her work has specifically focused on the Fourth Amendment and drone surveillance. She received her J.D. from New York Law School and her Bachelor's of Science degree from Florida State University.

Please go ahead.

STATEMENT OF AMIE STEPANOVICH, DIRECTOR, DOMESTIC SURVEILLANCE PROJECT, ELECTRONIC PRIVACY INFORMATION CENTER, WASHINGTON, DC

Ms. STEPANOVICH. Thank you, Chairman Leahy, Ranking Member Grassley, and members of the Committee, for your leadership in this area. In our statement today, EPIC recognizes that drones have tremendous positive uses in the United States. However, when drones are used to obtain evidence, intrude upon a reasonable expectation of privacy, or gather personal information about identifiable individuals, rules are necessary to ensure that fundamental standards for fairness, privacy, and accountability are preserved.

Recent records received by EPIC under the Freedom of Information Act demonstrate that the Bureau of Customs and Border Protection has outfitted drones with technology for electronic signals interception and human identification.

Law enforcement offices across the country have expressed interest in the purchase and use of drone technology. Records released show that law enforcement in Texas, Kansas, Washington, and other States are using drones. The Florida Police Chiefs Association has expressed interest in using drones for general crowd surveillance, and law enforcement in the State of Texas have expressed interest in using non-lethal weapons on drones.

As the Chairman has indicated, the privacy and security concerns arising from drones need to be addressed. State and local governments have considered a wide array of laws and regulations to prevent abuses associated with drone technology. But Congress can do more. EPIC offers the following recommendations on the best methods to provide the proper level of protection.

All drone operate should be required to submit detailed public reports on the drones' intended use. Issuance of a license should be contingent on the completion of these reports. And private right of action and other penalties should ensure compliance with what has been reported.

Warrant requirements should be mandated for law enforcement use of drones with narrow exceptions for exigent circumstances. And to further bolster the warrant requirement, broad and untargeted drone surveillance by law enforcement should be prohibited.

Drone operators should be prohibited from conducting surveillance of individuals that infringes on property rights. A Federal Peeping Tom statute, recognizing the enhanced capabilities of drones, would provide baseline privacy protection for individuals within the home. And all drone operators should be subject to third-party audits and oversight.

Thank you for the opportunity to testify here today, and I will be pleased to answer your questions.

[The prepared statement of Ms. Stepanovich appears as a submission for the record.]

Chairman LEAHY. Thank you very much.

Our next witness is Michael Toscano, who is president and CEO of the Association for Unmanned Vehicle Systems International, a nonprofit devoted exclusively to promoting unmanned systems. Previously he worked in the Office of the Deputy Assistant to the Secretary of Defense for Nuclear Matters. He has a Bachelor's of Science degree in both civil and environmental engineering from the University of Rhode Island.

And I should also note that once the vote starts, we are going to keep the hearing going, and we will be taking turns leaving. I think Senator Hirono is probably going to be the first to go vote, but we will keep it going so this can continue.

Go ahead, Mr. Toscano.

STATEMENT OF MICHAEL TOSCANO, PRESIDENT AND CHIEF EXECUTIVE OFFICER, ASSOCIATION FOR UNMANNED VEHICLE SYSTEMS INTERNATIONAL, ARLINGTON, VIRGINIA

Mr. TOSCANO. Good morning, Chairman Leahy and Ranking Member Grassley. I want to thank you and the rest of the members of the Judiciary Committee for inviting me to testify here today.

My organization, the Association for Unmanned Vehicle Systems International, or AUVSI, is the world's largest nonprofit organization devoted exclusively to advancing the unmanned systems and robotics community. We have more than 7,500 members, including more than 6,300 members in the United States. The industry is at the forefront of a technology that will not only benefit society, but also the U.S. economy. Earlier this month, my organization released a study, which found that the unmanned aircraft industry is poised to create 70,000 new jobs and $13.6 billion in economic impact within the first 3 years following the integration of unmanned aircraft into the national airspace.

However, the industry understands that this technology is new to most Americans, and their opinions are being formed by what they see in the news. Today's hearing is an excellent opportunity to address some misconceptions about the technology and discuss how it will actually be used domestically.

You have probably noticed that I do not use the term "drone." The industry refers to the technology as "unmanned aircraft systems," or UASes, because this is more than just a pilotless vehicle. A UAS also includes the technology on the ground, with a human at the controls. As I like to say, there is nothing unmanned about unmanned systems.

The term "drone" also carries with it a hostile connotation and does not reflect how UASes are actually being used domestically, as you heard from Mr. Miller. UASes are used to perform dangerous and difficult tasks more safely and more efficiently. They were used to assess flooding of the Red River in the upper Midwest. They were used to help battle wildfires in California. And they are being used to study everything from hurricanes in the Gulf of Mexico, tornadoes in the Great Plains, and volcanoes in Hawaii.

Unlike military UASes, the systems most likely to be used by public safety agencies are small systems that weigh less than 5 pounds, with limited flight duration. And you saw two examples here on the table. As for weaponization, it is a non-starter. The FAA prohibits deploying weapons on any civil aircraft. And for the record, AUVSI does not support the weaponization of civil UASes.

I also want to correct the misperception that there is no regulation of domestic UASes. The FAA strictly regulates who, where, when, and why unmanned aircraft will be flown. If a public entity wants to fly a UAS, they must obtain a Certificate of Authorization, or a COA, from the FAA. UASes are generally flown in line of sight of the operator, lower than 400 feet, and during daylight hours. It is currently a violation of FAA regulations to fly a UAS for commercial purposes.

As we focus on UASes for law enforcement, it is important to recognize the robust legal framework already in place, rooted in the Fourth Amendment of our Constitution and decades of case law——

Chairman LEAHY. And, Mr. Toscano, I do not mean to interrupt because you whole statement will be made part of the record, but we will have discussion of the Fourth Amendment and how it is involved. I appreciate you telling us what we should call them, but I think you leave that decision to us. We will decide what we will call them. You call them whatever you would like to call them.

Mr. TOSCANO. All right, sir.

Chairman LEAHY. We appreciate that very much.

[The prepared statement of Mr. Toscano appears as a submission for the record.]

Chairman LEAHY. Professor Ryan Calo is a professor at the University of Washington School of Law. He researches the intersection of law and emerging technology, co-chairs the Robotics and Artificial Intelligence Committee of the American Bar Association, is affiliate scholar at the Stanford Law School Center for Internet and Society, previously served as director.

Mr. Calo, please go ahead.

STATEMENT OF RYAN CALO, ASSISTANT PROFESSOR, UNIVERSITY OF WASHINGTON SCHOOL OF LAW, SEATTLE, WASHINGTON

Mr. CALO. Thank you, Chairman Leahy, Ranking Member Grassley, and members of the Committee, for this opportunity to testify today.

As you mentioned, I am a law professor. I am mostly here to answer your questions, and so I will not read my testimony that you have before you in the record. I just want to make a couple quick points by way of summary.

The first is that folks are very worried about the privacy ramifications of drones and that those concerns are well founded. Especially because drones drive down the cost of surveillance considerably, we worry that the incidence of surveillance will go up.

Americans' concerns are legitimate for another reason, which is that there is very little in American privacy law that would limit the domestic use of drones for surveillance, right? And so just a couple of examples of that.

There is no reasonable expectation of privacy in public or from a public vantage. Also, there is no reasonable expectation of privacy in contraband, and so the idea is that you can imagine drones flying around with chemical sensors—not the ones here on the table, but the ones that exist today and that the Department of Homeland Security and so on are looking into. They could fly around with chemical sensors looking for trace amounts of drugs and so forth.

The limits on private individuals—I realize this is obviously about law enforcement, but the limits on private individuals' use of drones are, if anything, probably fewer. And then you also have, as Senator Grassley mentioned, the issue of the First Amendment, which may in some way push back against limits on drones by the press.

So I think the best way to address this issue would be to finally drag our inadequate privacy doctrines into the 21st century, but I think that short of that, one stop-gap measure we should consider is that the FAA would actually kick the tires on privacy as part of its licensing process.

I do think we should be very careful about passing a national law restricting drones in particular because, actually, frankly, this inadequacy of privacy law is a problem that far outstrips just drones.

And with that, I would be very happy to take questions, and thanks again.

[The prepared statement of Mr. Calo appears as a submission for the record.]

Chairman LEAHY. Well, thank you, and I thank you for summarizing.

Mr. Miller, one, I appreciate you being here, especially as you are the manager of one of the only law enforcement programs in the country to operate a domestic drone. But I appreciate what you said about understanding constitutional safety and privacy concerns and so on.

Do you think it would ever be appropriate for a law enforcement agency to arm a drone with lethal weapons?

Mr. MILLER. Absolutely not. I think in the 4 years of research into our program, we have not seen a single thing that would present that as any tool that would be usable in our mission.

Chairman LEAHY. Do you get that same impression from your colleagues?

Mr. MILLER. Absolutely.

Chairman LEAHY. What about non-lethal weapons—tear gas, pepper spray, flash-bang grenades?

Mr. MILLER. You know, that has been brought up before. I can tell you that, in our experience, considering the risks of unmanned aircraft and then also the risks of use of less-than-lethal munitions, you know, such that they are, a bean bag round out of a shotgun, combining those two risks together is probably not the most responsible thing to do.

Chairman LEAHY. Now, I understand the drone you showed me there has a fairly short duration that it can be aloft. But do you think there would be drones law enforcement could use in the future, things like persistent surveillance or tracking, hours of surveillance or hours of tracking?

Mr. MILLER. What I can tell you now is that that is not affordable. Again, like I had commented before, why we use them is because they are affordable. They are cheap to operate.

As far as persistent surveillance, I can tell you that right now that capability is not new in unmanned aircraft. We can do a persistent surveillance mission with manned aircraft. But I can tell you the need for that is relatively low.

In fact, I can tell you in my 13 years I do not know of a persistent surveillance operation I have ever been a part of.

Chairman LEAHY. Technically, it would be feasible with a larger drone. Is that correct?

Mr. MILLER. Yes, that is what they are built for for the military.

Chairman LEAHY. Thank you.

And, Ms. Stepanovich, as drone technology and cameras and sensors become more advanced, I worry about not just the Government use of drones—and Mr. Miller has spoken very frankly on that—but the ability of private companies and individuals to intrude on the privacy of Americans. What do you see as the most significant—if you had to list one or two of the most significant privacy threats from the domestic use of drones, what would it be?

Ms. STEPANOVICH. The most significant trends in domestic use?

Chairman LEAHY. What are the most significant private threats from domestic use?

Ms. STEPANOVICH. One of them is going to be, I believe, what you had just mentioned, the persistent surveillance. Although Mr. Miller talked that there has never been a need for that, I think we saw in *United States* v. *Jones*, as the Ranking Member brought up in his opening remarks, that law enforcement has conducted persistent surveillance using other technologies, and that that is going to be a significant consideration as drone surveillance moves forward.

I also think, since the FAA is strictly prohibited from regulating model aircraft or individual use of drones, that there is going to be an issue with stalking, harassment, and other crimes using drones by individuals, and perhaps by corporations as well.

Chairman LEAHY. Does Congress have a role to play in this area?

Ms. STEPANOVICH. Yes, I do believe they have a significant role to play. As I mentioned in my opening statement, the States have looked extensively at drone surveillance laws, and at my last check over 30 States have introduced legislation on this issue. However, Congress can provide nationwide baseline privacy standards in order to ensure that individual rights and civil liberties are protected against drone surveillance.

Chairman LEAHY. Thank you. And, Professor Calo—and I also have a question for Mr. Toscano, but I notice my time is almost out, and I will submit that for the record. I would appreciate it if you would respond.

Professor Calo, you talked about Supreme Court cases regarding the constitutionality of aerial surveillance, which we have read. But do you believe that body of Supreme Court cases is adequate to guide the courts and law enforcement in the area of unmanned surveillance?

Mr. CALO. I am not sure that I even think they are adequate, you know, for purposes of manned surveillance. But with unmanned surveillance, there is an additional danger, that as the costs go down, you see more of it. And so, no, I am not sure that they are adequate. I think they need to be updated.

Chairman LEAHY. Thank you very much.

Senator Grassley.

Senator GRASSLEY. Professor Calo, the Supreme Court has held observation made while flying a manned aircraft in navigable airspace over a person's property does not violate the Fourth Amendment. In several cases, police were allowed to conduct surveillance over private property at heights ranging from 400 feet to 1,000 feet.

Question: How low must a drone fly over private property before it triggers a reasonable expectation of privacy or trespass under the Fourth Amendment? And what about if a drone would hover?

Mr. CALO. Sure. That is an excellent question, to which I am not sure I know the exact answer. It is true that if a drone were to trespass upon property, that would trigger the Fourth Amendment. And it used to be that you owned all the air rights, you know, all the way up into the heavens and all the way down. But, of course, after *Causby* and after commercial—the reality of commercial air flight, you can only own the property up to the air you could reasonably enjoy. So, certainly, if a drone were flying very close to your house, you could argue a trespass, but even if, you know, a few hundred feet above, probably would not.

As to hovering, I am not sure that there would be necessarily a distinction drawn between the capability of hovering or not. Obviously, *Florida* v. *Riley* is a helicopter case, and helicopters are capable of hovering in place, and so I am not sure that that would be seen as a distinction of constitutional moment.

Senator GRASSLEY. I want to ask Ms. Stepanovich about the same issue. How low do you think a drone can fly before impacting the Fourth Amendment?

Ms. STEPANOVICH. I agree with Mr. Calo's statement. The 400-foot mark was indicated by the Supreme Court because in that specific case that was the height that the helicopter in question was flying at. However, it is an open question on if lower aerial surveillance vehicles would be included in the reasonable expectation of privacy or the personal trespass.

Senator GRASSLEY. Then to the two of you again I will ask this question: Does the addition of technology such as facial recognition, biometric recognition, and thermal imaging equipment affect whether there is a reasonable expectation of privacy under the Fourth Amendment? First you and then you.

Mr. CALO. It does, and so we have a case involving thermal imaging where you needed a warrant or—at least it was a search for officers to look into your house and see intimate details. You know, one concern I have—and I think it is an open question—is if drones were to fly around and not actually feed images to law enforcement, but just detect chemicals or scan for unusual patterns, under the dog-sniffing cases, given that they are only looking for evidence of illegal activity, would that even trigger a search under the Constitution? And I think that is an open question and one that is teed up very well by drones.

Senator GRASSLEY. Ms. Stepanovich.

Ms. STEPANOVICH. The invasive technology that you listed that drones are designed to carry in many cases definitely will impact an individual's reasonable expectation of privacy.

In regard to the chemical sniffers that Mr. Calo discussed, there is technology now being developed by the Defense Department, DHS, and in use by the New York Police Department called "Terahertz Technology," and that can scan for chemical traces down to incredibly small traces that you may have come into contact with accidentally. And people can be triggered as potential targets based on those trace substances.

Senator GRASSLEY. Professor Calo, another question to you. If private individuals and commercial companies are allowed to use drones, for example, if utilities started using them to check meters or they obtained video on private property, are there limitations on whether law enforcement can obtain those videos absent a warrant?

Mr. CALO. Unless the officers instructed the private individuals to do the surveillance, then, no, they would not likely need a warrant for that. Obviously, the Fourth Amendment only applies to state actors.

There are some limitations that will apply to private parties and not to the Government, and so, for instance, there was an aerial surveillance case involving trade secrets that was thought to violate trade secret law even though it did not violate the Fourth Amendment.

Senator GRASSLEY. For Professor Calo, in regard to the First Amendment, I have several questions, but I will have to stop with this one. With regard to commercial applications, we have heard concerns about the increased use of private data collected by companies for advertising or other business purposes. What restrictions or limitations on private data collection by corporations exist?

Mr. CALO. Well, technically speaking, the First Amendment should not apply any differently to the press or corporations in terms of gathering information. Mostly it is about what people are allowed to say and so forth.

But there have been cases suggesting that you have a right, for instance, to photograph police in public, and so I think it is a mixed picture.

Senator GRASSLEY. OK. Thank you, Mr. Chairman.

Chairman LEAHY. Thank you.

Senator Feinstein.

Senator FEINSTEIN. Well, thank you very much, and I am one that has a real concern about drones being used commercially inside America. I know what drones can do, and, Mr. Toscano, you started out with a very seductive thing, and that is that it can produce large amounts of new jobs, which we would all like to have happen. However, I have seen drones do all kinds of things, and I think those all kinds of things bring on great caution.

I think we have to look to what purposes can drones be legitimately used. How do you monitor their use? How do you certify the equipment? Because all kinds of things can be added. It may well not be legal to carry any munitions on a drone, but what can be done illegally and how can the Government prevent that from happening?

I think the ability to—at what altitude can they fly? What kind of recognition, facial recognition, are they capable of at various activities? Can they take pictures of an individual through a window inside their home, a business through a window of their business, on the property on which they live? And drones are hard to spot for the untrained eye. So your ability to protect yourself is not great.

Mr. Miller, let me ask you this question: You have really outlined, I think, a very legitimate use for drones, which is a careful litany of law enforcement functions. I assume there are some forest fire issues for which you could use a drone as well. But you have been through the process to operate an unmanned aircraft. Can you describe the process? How rigorous is it? How long did it take your office to gain approval for its COA? And what conditions do you think should be placed on the granting of law enforcement use of drones?

Mr. MILLER. Absolutely. That is a wonderful question, and I think a key point of the conversation. The process was rigorous, it was long. It took us approximately 8 months to get the certificate that allows us to fly. That certificate allows us to fly daytime, only up to 400 feet off the ground, and we must remain within land sight.

Senator FEINSTEIN. Let me ask you, are your UAVs certified and are their remote pilots certified?

Mr. MILLER. That is a wonderful question, and the answer is no. And I think you are referring to an airworthiness certificate in public aviation. The airframe itself has been through a rigorous process to make sure that all the components that make up that aircraft are produced responsibly, out of good materials, et cetera, and they pass the test.

In this system here, that is not the case. None of the equipment on board here has passed the certification process to make sure that it is not going to fall out of the sky.

The approach that is taken is not one of certification of the aircraft but one of certification or risk mitigation of the operation. This system—and I say worst-case scenario, is it falling out of the sky, suddenly shutting off, which it never has—falling to the ground is relative low risk, for two reasons: one, it is 2 pounds and really cannot cause a lot of damage; but, two, we operate over defined incident perimeters, and we have that ability as law enforcement—and what I mean by—the best way to describe that is, you know, the "Police Line, Do Not Cross" kind of thing. If we are on a crime scene, you know, absolutely the public is not going to be walking through our crime scene that we are photo'ing. So we are over top of what we call only participatory people—that means our staff, they have safety equipment that they are using to make sure that it is a safe operation, and that is really the direction that the FAA has taken in allowing us to fly this equipment, because it is relatively low risk.

In the past, anytime we flew there was at least one life at risk, that being the pilot, if not more, and that is really not the case anymore.

Senator FEINSTEIN. Is there any regulation that indicates the distance you must keep from any airplane, whether it is commercial or private, small or large?

Mr. MILLER. Yes. Part 91 of the Federal Aviation Regulations have distances in place to stay away. Really, I think the issue here or the key here is that we cannot fly above 400 feet off the ground, and that is really kind of the lower limit for everybody else. In fact, in Class G airspace you cannot go below 500 feet off the ground, so there is a 100-foot buffer.

Senator FEINSTEIN. OK. My time is up.

Chairman LEAHY. Do you have something else you wanted to ask?

Senator FEINSTEIN. Well, I was going to ask Mr. Toscano, has anyone in the industry figured out how to create an unmanned aircraft that can safely detect, sense, and avoid other aircraft?

Mr. TOSCANO. The FAA right now has been mandated by September 2015 to assure integration of unmanned air systems into the national airspace. That is a safety requirement as we look at it. So sense and avoid or see and avoid for manned aircraft is an essential part. Technology is being developed today that will be certified at some point in time to assure that they are safe. And so because, as you have heard, there is a wide range of——

Senator FEINSTEIN. I am not talking about that. Perhaps you know. I am talking about the situation where a pilot landing in New York of a commercial jet said, "I see a drone." Do you know what that drone was, where it was from, and what it was doing there?

Mr. TOSCANO. The answer to that is no. I am not sure they have actually classified it of what it was. To my knowledge, they have not prudently or finally determined what it was that that pilot saw. I am not trying to be flippant here, but, you know, we talk about the sightings that are made all the time, and they are inaccurate. And until we find out the details, then in this particular case it could have been a model plane, it could have been other things that we do not know about at this point in time.

Senator FEINSTEIN. Thank you, Mr. Chairman.

Chairman LEAHY. Thank you.

Senator Lee.

Senator LEE. Thank you very much, Mr. Chairman.

Mr. Toscano, under of the FAA Modernization Reform Act of 2012, the FAA is required to establish unmanned aircraft system test ranges within the United States. I understand the FAA has requested proposals to create these test sites, and I also understand that Utah Valley University, which is the largest public University in my home State, is headlining an alliance that is one of the candidates for these sites.

Are you familiar with this aspect of the 2012 Act? And how do you see these sites and the testing that will be conducted there as contributing to the necessary regulations that we might need in the United States, including regulations related to privacy?

Mr. TOSCANO. That is an excellent question. This goes back to the responsibility of the FAA is to assure that anything that flies in the national airspace is safe. The only way that you can assure that safety is to test them. So these test sites that are being stated—there is one that already exists. It is in New Mexico State—and the six new ones that will be coming forward will have the capability to test to make sure that any unmanned air system will have the ability to operate safely into the national airspace. That is the design of those test sites, in which case they will certify the platform, the operator, in many cases the operational environment.

Senator LEE. You sound fairly confident that that will lead to some improvements, lead to any standards that need to be created, making sure that they are——

Mr. TOSCANO. Most definitely. If you look right now, they had 50 different entries that have been petitioned from 37 different States that are involved. The six that are identified right now in the FAA reauthorization bill that you quoted, those are being funded by the States themselves with certification from the FAA.

In the future, you may see that every State could have their own test site in order to be able to assure that the technology that is being deployed in the national airspace is, in fact, safe.

Senator LEE. OK. And then, Ms. Stepanovich, some proponents of drones, drone technology, have argued that current safeguards provide a significant protection of privacy, and they note that we have on the books related to the use of technology, you know, laws that we already have on the books related to use of other technologies that can overlap and include this type of technology certain remedies that provide civil remedies for violations of those laws.

Some have suggested that these legal protections should apply equally to drones, and that they may be sufficient to alleviate any constitutional problems or any privacy concerns.

In your view, is this approach correct? And what are the main differences between manned and unmanned aircraft as it relates to the protection of Americans for their privacy concerns and their rights under the Fourth Amendment?

Ms. STEPANOVICH. Thank you for the question. We do not believe that there are actually any Federal statutes that would provide limits on drone surveillance in the United States. The privacy laws that do exist are very targeted. It is the approach that the United States has taken to privacy, and they do not encompass the type of surveillance that drones are able to conduct. And because of this is why we are actually advocating for additional legislation on drone surveillance.

The primary difference between manned and unmanned vehicles is going to be—and I think this has been brought up—that drones are going to be able to conduct much more surveillance. They are cheaper to fly, cheaper to buy, cheaper to maintain, and, therefore, able to conduct an incredible amount more surveillance and subject individuals to the surveillance.

They are also designed, built and designed to carry some of the most invasive surveillance technology that is on the market today, and this further puts individuals at risk.

Senator LEE. I assume that part of your analysis in that has to do with the stealth factor by virtue of their size and the way many of them are operated. They do not make as much noise. They are harder to see. They are harder to hear. And they can move in and out, you know, like a thief in the night. You will not necessarily know that they are there. I assume that is one of the factors that significantly factors into your assessment on that front. Is that right?

Ms. STEPANOVICH. Yes, Senator.

Senator LEE. And then in your testimony, you mentioned several concerns that you have about drones. Even with current advancements, present-day technology and the cost of that technology places some real significant practical limitations on the use of drones. As Justice Alito discussed in a recent opinion, some of the most effective privacy protections are neither constitutional nor statutory but practical. But as technology advances, those practical limitations cease to act as an effective constraint on the privacy concerns that we are discussing here.

As you noted, the technology related to drones has developed much in the last decade, and it is going to continue to advance and make those same concerns even more significant.

One of my concerns relates to the coming years and the likelihood that those limitations will recede, along with the technological advances. In other words, as the technological advances make drones more effective and more cost-effective, these concerns can become more significant.

So, in your view, how should the potential for development of drone technology and the future uses of those systems affect our analysis here when we are examining the privacy implications of drone technology?

Ms. STEPANOVICH. I think the best thing to do, because of the incredible advancement of drone technology and where it is going to be—recently technologist Bruce Schneier said that today's rare and expensive is tomorrow's commonplace—is that we need legislation on this issue that is going to be technology neutral, and that means it is not going to become quickly outdated as technology increases. And this has been done in several laws in the past. If we look at the Electronic Communications Privacy Act, which is in the process of being updated now, many years late, it was able to hold through tremendous advances in technology and only recently is going to have to be—needs to be updated because of not being able to foresee the future of the Internet at that time. And I think it is important for all technology and privacy legislation to try to be as technology neutral as possible.

Senator LEE. Thank you.

Chairman LEAHY. Thank you. Thank you very much, Senator Lee. On the advance of technology, I referenced in my opening statement the theft done by Google of people's passwords and all. I mean, if somebody broke into your house and did that, you would want them arrested. They were doing it by driving by, and it was an egregious breach of people's privacy.

I am going to yield now to Senator Klobuchar. I have to go back to the floor because of the budget matters, but Senator Franken has offered to take the gavel, and I appreciate that, Senator Franken.

Senator Klobuchar.

Senator KLOBUCHAR. Thank you very much, Mr. Chairman. Thank you to all of you, and I do appreciate, being in Minnesota with the Red River Valley flooding and forest fires, those things that used the public safety use here. But I am concerned, as I hear more about the potential for individual citizens, for commercialization of this drone use, and also, obviously, some of the limits that were brought up even in the surveillance piece of this as well.

So my first question was just to follow up on Senator Feinstein where she was asking about—maybe Mr. Toscano and Mr. Miller—the safety issues in the airspace. And while I understand all this 400 feet and the limitations, if you started getting these in the hands of people that maybe did not quite know how to run them or something went wrong, what would happen—this is my simple question: What would happen if one of them came up against a small aircraft? Or would it matter? Or if you got a bigger drone? I mean, isn't there some safety concerns with that?

Mr. TOSCANO. When you look at the national airspace, there are rules and regulations that the FAA says you cannot fly anything within a certain distance of that airspace. If you do that, whether it is any type of machine, then you are violating the law, and there is a safety concern that you would be concerned about. That is why they have——

Senator KLOBUCHAR. I understand all that. I am just saying, What would happen if one of them hit a small plane? Like when birds hit a plane, it can create problems.

Mr. TOSCANO. In that case there, you can see what they are, and they range from 2 pounds up to very large type systems. And, yes, any incident where you have—there was a collision, then there could be damage.

Senator KLOBUCHAR. OK. Then the second piece of information is just, again, back to you, Mr. Calo, on just this commercialization, and I know someone asked you about it earlier, but what are the limits right now if someone wanted to just privately fly one?

Mr. CALO. Well, there are State statutes in some instances, and there is a common law privacy tort, intrusion upon seclusion, that says that if you really violate people's reasonable expectation of privacy—although you often have to do it repeatedly and you have to do it through outrageous conduct, then someone could sue you in civil court. There is an aerial surveillance case, at least one, involving trade secrets through aerial surveillance that came out in favor of the plaintiff.

Senator KLOBUCHAR. So someone could just buy one right now? Is that——

Mr. CALO. Well, you could go and buy——

Senator KLOBUCHAR. Would they have to get a certification from the FAA?

Mr. CALO. No, not really. So you could buy—I do not know if this stretches the limits to call it a drone, but you can buy something like a Parrot AR for about $300. It is an aerial vehicle that you can control with your iPad, and you could fly it around your neighborhood within line of sight, and unlikely you are not going to be running against any—you are not going to get sued over that in all likelihood.

The FAA, of course, does ban the commercial use of drones today, but that ban is set to be relaxed in 2015, and then we will, of course, have an economic incentive.

Incidentally, in my own personal view, to the extent you are interested, I think this is going to be a wonderful thing because I think this technology is deeply transformative, and I think that the—I think they are basically flying smartphones. And I think that one private industry gets their hands on these things, we are going to see some really great wonders.

However, we are never going to get there unless we place some limits and domesticate this problem of privacy. Because of our reactions to these drones, we are not going to avail ourselves of the technology.

Senator KLOBUCHAR. Ms. Stepanovich, how would you respond to that in terms of the issues in the hands of private commercialization?

Ms. STEPANOVICH. I think right now we are seeing already, even without commercial operators being legally able to operate drones, I think about every week, every month, I heard a story of the FAA having to go and shut down some commercial operator who is trying to take advantage of this technology before they are able to. So I think Mr. Calo is right that there are going to be incredible commercial uses of these. Google has already started using them actually to assist in their street view operations in other countries, not yet in the United States. So they are going to be used commercially, and I think that, as I said in my opening statement, creates new challenges as well.

Senator KLOBUCHAR. Senator Lee was asking about some of the technology and how that comes up against the laws and citing the Alito opinion. And according to the Congressional Research Service, some drones have facial recognition technology and radar, which can see through walls, in the same matter that airport security is used through layers of clothing.

What are some of these more advanced features of domestic drones? And how do you see this being developed? I guess I could ask you, Mr. Toscano.

Mr. TOSCANO. The technology that is being utilized on unmanned air systems is no different than the technology that exists today and can be used by manned systems. There is no technology leap that has taken place by the introduction of a UAS. What it allows you to do and the concerns that we are having that you might be able to do these sort of things at a very low cost and with a larger volume is the same things that cause the economic benefits with what we are seeing of the utilization.

So it is something that we have to address because there is a very huge upside to this technology, and because of that you cannot stop people from misusing any technology, just like you said, whether it is facial recognition, thermal imaging, or whatever. If they misuse it, the laws tell you that if you violate the laws, then you should be punished.

Senator KLOBUCHAR. I just do not think the laws have probably caught up with this new technology.

Mr. TOSCANO. And that may be the issue that we really should be discussing, is it is the technology that exists today, not the delivery system.

Senator KLOBUCHAR. Well, our laws need to be as sophisticated as the people that are potentially breaking them, so I think that is where we are headed to. So thank you very much.

Senator FRANKEN. [presiding.] Senator Cruz.

Senator CRUZ. Thank you, Mr. Chairman. Thank you to all of the witnesses for coming and testifying today.

It seems to me that drones are a technological tool that, as with most tools, can be used productively or can be abused. When we think about our conduct overseas, in particular in counterterrorism, I think drones have proven an effective tool in certain circumstances, and in particular have enabled us to deal with terrorists without placing servicemen and -women directly in harm's way.

At the same time, it seems to me that overseas our conduct needs to be consistent with the laws of war, and domestically in the United States that our conduct in all circumstances needs to be consistent with the Constitution. And how that applies to drone surveillance or, a topic for another day, use of lethal force is not necessarily an easy question.

I would like to begin, Mr. Miller, with a question for you, which is: Are there limitations on the uses of drones that your members would support as common-sense protections of the privacy of American citizens?

Mr. MILLER. The easy answer is yes. We already looked to case law. One of the things that we have positioned our program on, or the concept is that we have not really invented a new ability to collect information. You know, the camera has done that for us. It has done that for us in decades, you know, in the past, and so there is case law out there that speaks to the direction which we take when we consider putting a camera in the air.

You know, really, the fact that it flies on this size system or, you know, the typical police helicopter you see really has not changed the way we think about it or view it.

Senator CRUZ. So what limitations would your members support?

Mr. MILLER. Let me clarify. I think the limitations that we would support are the ones that we currently have identified through the study of case law that has occurred to this time.

Senator CRUZ. It seems to me that there should be an important distinction between individuals for whom there is probable cause, substantial evidence to be suspected of a crime, and law enforcement has always had extensive tools for operating in that environment, and the collection of data concerning ordinary citizens. When you overlay the availability of drones with the proliferation of things such as stationary cameras—I will note my hometown of Houston recently voted to take down red light cameras. I think a great many of us, myself included, have very deep concerns about the Government collecting information on the citizenry. And with the ease and availability of drones, I think there is a real concern that the day-to-day conduct of American citizens going about their business might be monitored, catalogued, and recorded by the Federal Government. And then I for one would have very deep concerns about that.

I would ask a question of Ms. Stepanovich. Do you share those concerns? And if so, what reasonable limitations should be considered to protect the privacy rights of all Americans?

Ms. STEPANOVICH. I think anytime when you come up with a new surveillance technology, you are going to have instances where the technology catches bad actors doing bad deeds. However, if those few instances are at the expense of Dragnet constant surveillance of all citizens as they go about their daily lives, it is not consistent with our constitutional protections and what our country was built on.

I think we need to prevent drones from becoming alternatives for police patrols flying up and down or in some instances, when you are not talking about aerial drones, driving up and down the street collecting all sorts of information about individuals, supplemented by the facial recognition technology, the automatic license plate readers. I think we do need to enforce a warrant requirement for drones in circumstances where they are collecting criminal evidence, and I think we need to address, in addition to law enforcement use, also commercial and individual uses of drones.

Senator CRUZ. Mr. Toscano.

Mr. TOSCANO. Senator, I think that is the core of the issue that we have here today. The conversation should be focused on what is the Government's right to collect, to use, to store, to disseminate, to share information.

Last year, we put out a Code of Conduct that says this is how you should use UASes in order to get the benefit and to make sure that you do not violate the privacy of an individual. The IACP, the International Association of Chiefs of Police, put out their guidelines and which the ACLU has applauded as being the good guidelines in order how to use this technology.

There is a tremendous opportunity for this technology to be used, and it is not a different type of surveillance. The technology is the same technology that exists today. It is how it is being used. And I understand the benefits that you get from having a low-cost, reliable capability that can provide you with the ability to move a mission package payload from one point to another. But what you do with that and the human being that is involved in it is the one that is responsible. Just because there is not a pilot in the plane, the individual that is operating that platform is still responsible. And if that person uses it in an incorrect way or misuses it, then that person should be held accountable.

Senator CRUZ. Thank you, Mr. Chairman.

Senator FRANKEN. Thank you.

Senator Hirono.

Senator HIRONO. Thank you, Mr. Chairman, and to all of the panelists.

Professor Calo, I think you are the person who mentioned that the Fourth Amendment only applies to state actors, and so at least there are protections against unreasonable Government intrusion. So my concern really centers around what happens when non-state actors can utilize this technology? And after 2015 apparently the sky is the limit. Do you think that Congress has the power to prohibit private citizens and corporations from using drones with cameras that are capable of storing images? Or, in fact, what is the limit to what Congress can do to provide limitations on non-state actors and their use of drones?

Mr. CALO. Yes, I think that Congress can provide those limits. Again, the First Amendment draws a distinction between stopping someone from talking about something and general prohibitions. So, for instance, the Government may say that you are not allowed to do X, Y, and Z in order to gather information in the first instance, and that can apply across the same way to the press or individuals, whoever else they might be. And so as a consequence, yes, they probably can.

Now, that said, they would not be able to make sort of content-based kind of distinctions about who can use drones and who cannot. But setting basic privacy limits for everybody to use drones will apply in equal measure to individuals in the press and so forth. And so, yes, I think Congress does have that capability.

Senator HIRONO. Well, it is coming up with what constitutes these basic privacy limitations. That is the rub, right?

Mr. MILLER. Yes.

Senator HIRONO. It is not going to be so easy to come up with that kind of language.

With this technology changing as fast as we can probably sit here talking about this, I was intrigued with Ms. Stepanovich—when you said that any laws that we propose should be technology neutral, I am very intrigued by that. What would you consider a technology-neutral way to set some limits on the private use of drones?

Ms. STEPANOVICH. I think the best way is to look at the surveillance that drones can conduct, looking at data retention and data minimization, and making sure that no individual has kind of persistent data bases of information collected on them.

One of the great places we have to turn are the Fair Information Practices, which have been incorporated by the OECD in their guidelines to look for what protections need to be in place whenever information is collected about individuals.

Senator HIRONO. So, Ms. Stepanovich, perhaps other panel members could weigh in on this, too, but I would think that it would be pretty difficult to enforce these kinds of statutes for law enforcement. For example, you know, if we establish some parameters, geographic parameters or height parameters or visual sighting parameters, who is supposed to enforce whether all of these limitations are being met?

Ms. STEPANOVICH. Some of the things that we have asked for include audits that would reveal when possible violations are occurring, and private rights of action, so individuals who observe drones being operated in a way that they are not supposed to be or allowed to be can actually bring suit against the drone operator.

However, I want to note that at least a Federal statute would be enforceable. Mr. Toscano brought up the AUVSI guidelines and the chiefs of police guidelines. The AUVSI guidelines have one line in them about privacy. The chiefs of police guidelines are a little more protective. However, neither of those are enforceable provisions, and I think that we——

Senator HIRONO. Do you think a private cause of action—and I could ask Professor Calo also—in this area might be a very important part of any law that we propose?

Ms. STEPANOVICH. Yes.

Mr. CALO. I am not sure where I come down on that. I think there are couple of dangers of legislating at the Federal level, and maybe one approach to think about is to allow the States to come up with individual ways of doing things and see whether the common law torts can also adapt to changing circumstances.

So I am not sure I come down one way or the other about whether there is a good idea of a private cause of action. I do think that some safeguards are absolutely necessary because otherwise I think Americans are going to reject this technology which could be very beneficial.

Senator HIRONO. Thank you. My time is up.

Senator FRANKEN. Senator Blumenthal.

Senator BLUMENTHAL. Thank you, Mr. Chairman.

Let me pursue the question that arises from your last response, if I may, and ask you whether, in fact, if there is legislation, shouldn't it be at the Federal level because we are dealing with an industry which is Federal in scope, issues that pertain to air safety? Obviously, the FAA has a mandate to provide for integration by 2015 because of the prospect of 30,000 or more of these UAVs, drones, whatever you want to call them, flying around in our airspace. Isn't this sort of quintessentially an issue for Federal regulation if there is going to be legislation?

Mr. CALO. The short answer is I just do not know. I mean, I completely agree with respect to safety that, of course, FAA has expertise, it has its own integrated approach. I also support as a stopgap the idea of asking the Federal Aviation Administration to consider privacy as one of the prerequisites to issuing licenses. I think that all makes a lot of sense.

I do think that there is some benefit of the fact that the States are laboratories of ideas, and so you have some States which say, look, anything goes here, and other States that say nothing goes here; and maybe we will learn from that experience. And that is all I am trying to say.

Senator BLUMENTHAL. And I agree as a former State law enforcement official that States sometimes are much better equipped and able to deal with these kinds of questions, and I think at a certain level very likely States can safeguard privacy concerns, establish standards that are then proven or disproved in the laboratory as—I think it was Justice Frankfurter referred to them as the "laboratory for legal development."

Do you know of any challenges that are ongoing now—and any of the members of the panel can respond—challenges either to private practices or law enforcement actions pending in the courts or planned? And maybe I should begin with Ms. Stepanovich. You would probably know.

Ms. STEPANOVICH. I know of one right now. Customs and Border Protection has an ongoing program where they allow State and local law enforcement and other Federal agencies to borrow their Predator B drones and use them to conduct surveillance that is not related to the Customs and Border Patrol mission. This is something that EPIC has been pursuing, and we are submitting today a petition to Customs and Border Protection for them to suspend this practice. However——

Senator BLUMENTHAL. You are submitting it today?

Ms. STEPANOVICH. Today. However, North Dakota, this practice has already been used to conduct surveillance of a suspected and alleged cattle thief who was holed up on his property. They flew the drone over his property and collected information about him and used that information to arrest him. It is the first use of a drone to arrest a U.S. citizen on U.S. soils.

Senator BLUMENTHAL. And the courts really could be relied on to protect privacy in the law enforcement setting except almost certainly those cases will arise in the context of efforts to exclude evidence in a criminal prosecution rather than, let us say, surveillance or monitoring or other potentially invasive activities that might not result in the prosecution where a motion to exclude evidence would be filed.

Ms. STEPANOVICH. Exactly, and we believe that we need the protections in advance of getting to that stage in the prosecution. When a court challenge has already been brought to exclude evidence or for surveillance issues, that means that rights have already been violated. And we think that legislative efforts could put protections in place to prevent that from ever happening.

Senator BLUMENTHAL. Well, my general view is that we need to update the law. Clearly there is a need for everyone's interest to update the law, if only to provide the industry with the kind of bright lines and standards it needs and deserves to develop and apply this new technology. I am amazed that the case that is sought by all sides for reliance as to the doctrines applicable here is a 1986 case involving aerial surveillance from an airplane where the U.S. Supreme Court upheld that practice by law enforcement officials, and here we have an entirely new, advancing, fast-changing, potentially very intrusive technology, but also with very positive uses as well, if properly channeled.

So I hope that whether it is State courts and State law or Federal courts in advance of legislation or Federal agencies, the FAA, for example, issuing permits and applying privacy standards, can somehow develop doctrines that update our current constitutional principles and safeguard privacy, which is very much in need of protection, not only in the collection of data but also retention and distribution. For me, the issues are not only what private companies or the Government does to collect data, but also how they retain it, how they store it, how they keep it, and what they do with it—selling, exchanging, disseminating it.

So thank you, Mr. Chairman.

Senator FRANKEN. Thank you, Senator.

Senator Durbin.

Senator DURBIN. Thank you, Mr. Chairman.

As Chair of the Privacy Subcommittee, Senator Franken takes up these issues with some frequency, and I am reminded that when I first came to this Committee, someone noted that the word "privacy" cannot be found in our Constitution. But we have established that right, and I believe most of us believe it is a very important right that we cherish and want to protect, and that is what this conversation is about.

We are trying to take a document, the Constitution in this case, written many years ago and apply it to the modern world, and at times we have had to struggle with that. The telephone was beyond anyone's imagination when the Constitution was written. The Internet and all of the trafficking that goes on through computers 20 or 30 years ago was unthinkable. And I will tell you, serving as Chairman of a Subcommittee that deals with the military and our intelligence operations, the capacity that we have for surveillance is dramatically improving, and we are using it to our benefit to keep America safe. And I am glad that we are. We may lead the world in that category. I want us to continue to.

But when it comes to this emerging technology, the challenge has been discussed here at length on this Committee—the intersection of our personal privacy and the march of technology, and what we need to do by way of law or policy to really face it.

Professor Calo, cases that you noted in your testimony really, as you said, are not right on point. More or less the Supreme Court is talking about GPS detection of a suspect, thermal imaging, and the like. So it appears to me that there is more to be said when it comes to the question of our civil liberties, the prosecution of a crime, and the use of this technology. What do you think are the major elements that are still out there unresolved in these court decisions?

Mr. CALO. There is a tremendous amount of flexibility in the doctrine, and so at its core, what we are talking about is whether someone has a subjective expectation of privacy that then society is prepared to accept as reasonable. And so what we have is a bunch of data points saying that if someone flies over your house or your company or whatever it happens to be, with a helicopter or a plane, that your expectation of privacy vis-a-vis people in national airspace is not reasonable. Or we have cases suggesting that affixing a GPS device to a vehicle is technically a trespass and, hence, is a search under the Constitution and so forth.

So I agree that they are not directly on point, but they——

Senator DURBIN. Well, what about red light cameras? I am driving through this intersection and did not even know it, there is a red light camera that is monitoring my conduct and may end up taking a photograph and sending me a ticket in a week or two.

Mr. CALO. Yes, I mean, I think that there are real dangers there, but I think the current constitutional doctrine will not capture that. That is to say, I do not think that that is going to be seen as violating the Fourth Amendment. And I do not think that most uses of drones are going to be seen as violating the Fourth Amendment. And that is potentially really the problem, which is that not just drones but surveillance technology has vastly outpaced privacy law, in my view, and it needs updating.

One of the dangers of regulating in this space and limiting the regulation to unmanned aircraft systems is that there are other things, like traffic cameras; you know, there are robots that climb the side of a building. Would those be captured by an unmanned aircraft system? I think it is more of an updating all of privacy law to reflect contemporary technology.

Senator DURBIN. So, Mr. Miller, you are in the law enforcement field. Let us follow through on that. Currently there are efforts underway in many communities, not all, to collect this information from just the general conduct of the population. Now, do you see that as a parallel to the use of drones?

Mr. MILLER. No, I do not think as a parallel. I think you speak to really the issue at hand is the information. As I am listening to Professor Calo, I am thinking about medical information. And I think what we are doing today, the conversation is centered around a tool as if medical information and the protections that protect my medical information matters that a doctor collects it, maybe asks that hard question, and a nurse does not. Or, you know, the physician's assistant is only allowed to ask me these questions or what they do with the information.

I think in this conversation it is very important to focus on the information. I can tell you that that is where my agency stands, is to focus on the information. It is the information—it does not matter how we collect it. It is what we do with it, how we maintain that public trust with the public by not taking the photo of you in the traffic infraction and putting it on the front page of the paper.

Senator DURBIN. So let me just challenge you on that point. It is not a matter of how we collect but what we do with it. What about the right to be left alone, which is really kind of basic in America? You know, and whether we are talking law enforcement on one side, the private sector on another, just generally collecting information about my life.

Mr. MILLER. I think you make a great point, but, again, I think it is—you bring that question about, you know, I just want to be left alone, or that comment, and you bring that back to—it is not really just law enforcement, but what can we collect, and once we have, what can we do with it?

Senator DURBIN. So, Professor Calo, this common law tort that you talked about, it is the first time I had ever heard of it. What is it again?

Mr. CALO. Intrusion upon seclusion.

Senator DURBIN. That is alliterative. And how often has it been tested? I mean, is this an established tort?

Mr. CALO. It is an established tort. In fact, it was—the intellectual underpinnings are the same as the right to be left alone, so it is an 1890 Law Review article that has been very influential sort of sets out the elements that are later codified or adopted by other courts.

It is not tested all the time. Part of the reason is that the conduct at issue has to be pretty outrageous for it to trigger, and that is because, you know, all of us are going around looking at one another all the time, and so you want to be able to have a threshold that gets met.

I do, though, tend to agree that there really is a subjective element of harm to being—living in a society where you feel like you are under surveillance. So irrespective of whether the data is being collected or shared, just feeling like you are living under drones could have that effect if there are no safeguards in place.

Senator DURBIN. Mr. Chairman, I wish we had more time here, and I thank the panel for their contribution. I will tell you that——

Senator FRANKEN. Just go ahead and take as much time as you want.

Senator DURBIN. No. I have to leave, unfortunately, but I want to mention that after Easter recess, we are going to have a hearing in the Subcommittee on the Constitution about the use of drones in an international context. I am glad Senator Leahy kicked this off with Senator Franken, but it will get into the whole question of the lethal use of drones, the law of war, and the Constitution, which is another challenging area of the law. But I thank you for this hearing. It is timely and very important.

Senator FRANKEN. Thank you, Senator.

As Senator Durbin said, I am Chairman of the Subcommittee on Privacy, Technology, and the Law, and this sort of seems like this hearing could have been held in that Subcommittee. I am glad we did it as the whole Committee.

This is the perfect example of why I believe there is—I would characterize the Constitution as "a living Constitution." The Founders, I think it would be fair to say, probably did not anticipate this. They did not anticipate the phone, and that is why at a certain point we had to decide whether phone taps were a violation of the Fourth Amendment. And that really came down to people's expectation of privacy, and that is kind of a big part of what we are talking about here today.

Look, there is no question that this technology has unbelievable potential for law enforcement, for legitimate law enforcement, for commercial applications, certainly no one would argue with agricultural applications, no one would argue for mining or for—there are all kinds of unbelievable uses of this, but we do have these privacy concerns.

I guess one of my questions is about who should oversee this, who exactly—I will start with Ms. Stepanovich. Last year, the Government Accountability Office, told us that, "No single Federal agency has been statutorily designated with specific responsibility to regulate privacy matters." But what they were referring to related to domestic drones.

There is disagreement on whether that responsibility should be centralized in one body, and if so, which agency could do it the most effectively.

In your opinion, what type of oversight would most effectively protect Americans' civil liberties, their privacy when it comes to UAS?

Ms. STEPANOVICH. Mr. Calo has mentioned a couple times that there is a stop-gap with the FAA's oversight and licensing authority. EPIC recognized that back in February 2012 after the FAA Act was passed and petitioned the FAA to implement privacy regulations as part of their process to increase the use of drones in the United States. We believe that the FAA does have a critical role to play in this by mandating as a contingent on licensing for drone operators to turn over information about what surveillance operations they are going to conduct and to make that information publicly available and to hold them accountable to sticking to that information. So we think that the FAA is the primary regulating source.

We also believe that when other entities choose to operate drones, such as Customs and Border Protection or the Department of Justice, they need to implement privacy regulations and surveillance limitations within their own use of drones, subject to notice and comment rulemaking.

Senator FRANKEN. I am not quite sure then who is overseeing that, if there is a single agency. Mr. Toscano.

Mr. TOSCANO. If we have a privacy concern or debate right now today, where would you go for that? You would not go to the FAA. They have very limited, if any, expertise in the area of privacy. What they do have and what is mandated by them is they are responsible for safety. Anything that flies in the national airspace can only be done by virtue of the granting of the FAA saying that it is done in a safe manner. And that is the responsibility of the FAA, and that is a tremendous responsibility that we take in high regard. So I think we should let the FAA do what they do best.

And when you talk about privacy, I am very fortunate to have lawyers to the left and to the right of me, and actually in front of me and in back of me. Those are the individuals——

Senator FRANKEN. Very fortunate indeed.

Mr. TOSCANO. Yes.

[Laughter.]

Mr. TOSCANO. Those are the individuals—and as we have talked about today, this is about privacy in general. This is about the concern of gathering information, how it is used, how it is stored, how it is disseminated, and how it is destroyed. That is done through a different framework.

And so I look to this and say that is the essence of what we are talking about, and it will come down from law. Whether it comes from State Peeping Tom laws or whether it comes from the Constitution or the Fourth Amendment, which is based on——

Senator FRANKEN. You are talking about legislation.

Mr. TOSCANO. Correct.

Senator FRANKEN. And the legislation by necessity will kind of appoint some agency to oversee this, I would think. And who should that be, Professor? Or is it not one agency, centralized in one agency?

Mr. CALO. There is economic scholarship, at least that I have read, suggesting that we are faring relatively well with the multiple hats approach here. Also, I confess that I am not convinced that Federal legislation is the right move at this time.

I will disagree with Mr. Toscano about the FAA. I mean, it is true historically that the FAA has looked at safety, but I do not see any reason why the FAA could not gain expertise around privacy.

I received a letter from the FAA——

Senator FRANKEN. Now, the FAA did tell GAO that this was not—they have no expertise on privacy.

Mr. CALO. That is true. I recall them telling GAO that, but then only in February, I received a letter from the FAA saying, "We would like your input on how we should think about privacy in connection to testing centers." And so the truth of the matter is I think that the FAA is capable of gaining expertise, as any agency is, and that they could be a good repository.

Senator FRANKEN. OK. Well, we will keep thinking about that.

There has been some testimony and talk about questions about or mention of data retention and dissemination. What are the issues and who would be overseeing that? In other words, again, is that a legislative responsibility? And would we be talking about a privacy law regarding UAV or UAS information?

Mr. CALO. The Privacy Act actually does place some limits on sharing among agencies and with the public of private, personally identifiable information with respect to Government actors.

Senator FRANKEN. I am sorry to interrupt you, but we have smartphones now, and someone referred to this as a flying smartphone.

Mr. CALO. That was me, yes.

Senator FRANKEN. OK. Well, we are having a little bit of a problem, you know, in that regard, trying to put our finger on exactly how we regulate that.

Mr. CALO. Senator, you are preaching to the converted on this issue. You know, I think that the FTC and the FCC have struggled mightily, not just with, you know, the network and the device itself, but all the apps on top of it. It is a little bit of a mess.

I am not sure that we will fare any better around drones. I think that perhaps it is a matter of triage. If we want to avail ourselves of this technology, as many here agree we should, then perhaps we should have at least something in place so Americans feel more comfortable. And I think that the most obvious authority for that right now is the FAA, although, again, I believe that, you know, we really should be updating Fourth Amendment law in general to deal with contemporary surveillance technology.

Senator FRANKEN. Speaking of flying smartphones, I am just interested in—I mean, we are now talking about technology that obviously we have not talked about until now and we certainly would not have been talking about 10 years ago. So I am wondering about nanotechnology. You know, I think people would probably have been surprised before this hearing to see that that is what—that is a UAV, OK, and that is what we are talking about in large part.

How small can these things get? And I think maybe the answer to that is we do not know, and a thousand years from now, I bet you they will be smaller, and we may just be brains on a thing. So never mind that.

[Laughter.]

Senator FRANKEN. Let us not go there.

But what we are talking about here in terms of the capabilities here are obviously—I will go to Ms. Stepanovich. You get to handle this. You are talking about technology neutral, but we are going to have—this technology is just going to exponentially get more sophisticated and probably smaller, don't you think?

Ms. STEPANOVICH. I do believe so, and one of the major images we think of when we think of drones are the big Predator drones, which are being operated in the United States. But we also have the ones that you see on the desk in front of you all the way down to there are now drones the size of a humming bird being developed, and micro drones and drones even smaller. So the technology is increasing at an exponentially rapid rate, and as we move forward, we are just going to see the capabilities of these devices increase.

Senator FRANKEN. So presumably at some point you could have one the size of a mosquito that has a battery that operates for weeks, and you could have a mosquito following you around and not be aware of it.

Ms. STEPANOVICH. There are already images online of a mosquito drone being developed by the National Security Agency and them trying to figure out what technology they can put on it, to make small enough to put on it.

Senator FRANKEN. God help us if an adolescent boy gets a hold of one of those.

[Laughter.]

Senator FRANKEN. Mr. Toscano.

Mr. TOSCANO. You know, there was——

Senator FRANKEN. I do not know what that meant, by the way.

[Laughter.]

Mr. TOSCANO. Obviously, we have had tremendous advancement in technology over the last couple hundred years, and we can continue to understand how that may go forward. A lot of that is due to different properties that have happened in processing capabilities and things of that nature. But the figure was used before that the FAA said there would be 30,000 of these flying in the airspace. Well, that was an earlier figure. They have now revised that to say about 10,000.

But if you looked at what those 10,000 might be, they are not going to be 10,000 surveilling drones that are just following Americans. If you look at the report we did, 80 percent of the application is going to be in farming, in precision agriculture. And if you look at it from a public safety standpoint—and that includes the law enforcement which talked today, but also firefighters, first responders, things of this nature—you are going to see that that is a small quantity in the bigger picture. And, you know, when Ms. Stepanovich mentioned about one that was used in order to go over a rancher's facility, that was called in by State entities to a Federal request. It could have been done with a manned system. They could have done it with a helicopter. But the technology was there and available, and they took advantage of it.

So I guess the point we are making is that we seem to be fixated on the truck or the what-if of this thing could be happening. But like I say, we have already talked about it. It is the law of—the privacy aspect of the information that is being collected. That is what is key and critical. And that is something that we are going to have to keep dealing with as not just this technology. Fifty years ago, we had this thing called the Internet that came out of the military, and there were many hearings just like this that were concerned about the privacy of this thing called the Internet, that you were going to put your personal data on this thing, and you would be connected to all these different entities without having any measures in place.

Well, 50 years later, here we are and the Internet is an integral part. It has helped us tremendously with the gross national product of our Nation and in the world. It has made our lives better. Are there misuses of the Internet? Well, I think we can all attribute to that and understand that that is a true statement. But we now have, what, bullying laws that have come up that say because someone is misusing this technology, we have to put the right legislation or the right parameters in place to make sure that we get to take advantage of all the upside, which is a huge upside, and still make sure that it is protected.

Senator FRANKEN. I think no one is questioning the commercial potential and the public safety potential and the public good that can come from this. But we are—you know, one of my big duties here in the Senate is to look out for people's privacy, and I see that Professor Calo wanted to respond.

Mr. CALO. Thank you, Senator. I appreciate it.

I just wanted to use the Internet analogy and say that when we first deployed the commercial Internet, there were many people that were very nervous about using it. They did not want to go on there and do transactions online. And we had to get security adequate enough so that people felt comfortable using the Internet so that it can be what it is today.

The same has to be said about drones. If we are going to realize the commercial potential of drones, we are going to need to get these privacy and civil liberties issues right.

Senator FRANKEN. Safeguards will enhance the ability to use them in the correct way.

Mr. CALO. Correct. And we concur. That is what is needed.

Senator FRANKEN. One last thing that came up, and then we will bring this to an end. Ms. Stepanovich, facial recognition has been brought up, and when I started to talk about the technological development of these, I mean, is there fear that this can be used in a way—and, again, the fear is that we kind of have to address in order to make sure that we are able to use them properly—that there will be—that use of facial recognition—and not just in the hands of law enforcement or the Government, but also in the hands of private entities, and what possible misuse could this be put to?

Ms. STEPANOVICH. I do not think there is as much fear as a realistic expectation that this is going to be deployed on drones. We have already seen reports that it is being developed, and both commercial and public entities wishing to deploy it on drones.

Facial recognition technology comes with its own risks because it totally connects an individual's life. You can keep a full picture of what happens to an individual throughout the day, not only in their public life but on their online transactions. You can connect those kind of two separate worlds once you start deploying facial recognition information.

So this technology in the hands of commercial and Government operators on drones increases the kind of surveillance picture for what drones are going to be able to collect.

Senator FRANKEN. And could give everyone the sense essentially of having no privacy whatsoever in their lives.

Ms. STEPANOVICH. Yes.

Senator FRANKEN. Which is a tremendous loss. So we have to make sure that we can handle that through the law so that we can do the positive uses of this technology.

Thank you all for your time and for your testimony. I think it has been a very productive hearing, and it is clear to me that the tremendous potential of this technology to create jobs and reduce costs for law enforcement operations cannot be overstated. But it is also clear that there are serious privacy and civil liberties concerns felt by all the members of this Committee. We need to be doing more to prevent drones from being used in an abusive manner that violates Americans' privacy rights, and I think only if we do this, to follow up on Professor Calo, then that will allow us to do the commercial applications and only if we do that properly.

This hearing has been an important first step toward explaining these complex issues, and I hope this panel will continue to work with me, all of you, and other members of this Committee on appropriate legislation to address the privacy concerns discussed today. Thank you all again for your testimony.

The hearing record will stay open for a week if anyone would like to submit additional statements or questions. This meeting is adjourned. Thank you all.

[Whereupon, at 12:24 p.m., the Committee was adjourned.]

[Questions and answers and submissions for the record follow.]

[Additional material is being retained in the Committee files, see contents.]

QUESTIONS AND ANSWERS
SCHOOL OF LAW
UNIVERSITY of WASHINGTON

April 10, 2013

Senators,

Thank you for your insightful questions about the law and policy that attend the domestic use of drones, and again for inviting me to testify on this important issue. I have provided some initial answers below and would be happy to continue the conversation at the Committee's convenience.

Sincerely,

Ryan Calo
Assistant Professor
University of Washington School of Law

SCHOOL OF LAW
UNIVERSITY of WASHINGTON

QUESTIONS FROM RANKING MEMBER CHARLES GRASSLEY

Question 1.A: Does the reasoning in *Jones* or *Jardines* change the analysis for reviewing aerial surveillance by unmanned systems of the Fourth Amendment?

Maybe. *Jones* signals a willingness on the part of a majority of Justices (five of nine) to revisit the doctrine that citizens enjoy no reasonable expectation of privacy in public, whereas *Jardines* suggests that drug or bomb-sniffing drones would not be subject to the Fourth Amendment unless they were to fly so low as to interfere with property rights.

Technically *Jones* holds that attaching a GPS device to a vehicle for the purpose of gathering information and without the citizen's permission constitutes a search. As drones can follow a car without touching it, the majority opinion would not seem to control. Yet five Justices, over several concurrences, worried aloud about following a citizen in public by electronic means and suggested that such surveillance might trigger Fourth Amendment scrutiny if sufficiently extensive.

Jardines, meanwhile, holds that bringing a police dog within the curtilage of a home (in this case, the front porch) constitutes a search for purposes of the Fourth Amendment. We may tacitly consent to officers coming to knock on our front door to ask a question, but we do not, the Court reasoned, tacitly consent to bringing an instrumentality of investigation onto our property.

But now please assume no trespass or "intrusion" onto a citizen's property. Imagine a drone equipped with the ability to detect unlawful chemicals that flies over a public street or high above the suspect's house. In that case, I would think that *at least* Justice Thomas, who was in the majority in *Jardines*, would move over and join the four-Justice dissent, creating a five to four opinion finding no search because citizens enjoy no reasonable expectation of privacy in contraband (*Illinois v. Caballes*).

Question 1.B: Does the low cost and effort associated with drone surveillance change the Fourth Amendment calculus?

It may. Again, five Justices in *Jones* evinced a concern over how easy it had become to follow people around in public using electronic means.

W SCHOOL OF LAW
UNIVERSITY of WASHINGTON

Question 1.C: Does the addition of technology, such as facial recognition, biometric recognition, and thermal imaging equipment affect whether there is a reasonable expectation of privacy?

Facial and biometric recognition underscore the shortcomings of the doctrine that citizens possess no reasonable expectation of privacy in public. The same Justices I've mentioned in *Jones* might be prepared to accept as reasonable (*Katz* test) an expectation of privacy against drones or even linked cameras that can re-identify individuals using facial recognition. These technologies and others (e.g., license plate readers) make it possibly to follow someone around electronically without committing much in the way of manpower.

I believe the Supreme Court's decision in *Kyllo* puts thermal imaging in its own category. The use of thermal imaging to detect activity within a private space likely requires a warrant or else must qualify under a limited exception. On the other hand, the use of thermal imaging merely to detect bodies in public at night probably would not. It might also be that thermal imaging is today in widespread enough use that the Court would revisit whether citizens are reasonable in not expecting it. (A company called Essess, for instance, drives around taking thermal images of people's houses.)

Question 2.A: Does the First Amendment prohibit Congress from restricting the use of drone technology by the press?

As I understand the relevant doctrine, the First Amendment generally tolerates restrictions on data collection activities as long as they are reasonable and apply to everyone equally. Congress probably could not single out the press for a ban on drone photography. But even today, the press may not fly drones because of Federal Aviation Administration rules that apply to all private entities excepting hobbyists.

Question 2.B: What reasonable restrictions could Congress considering placing on the use of drones by the press?

I would think any press-specific limits on the use of drones could be constitutionally problematic. Even California's anti-paparazzi law—recently upheld in state court against a challenge to its constitutionality—is grounded in trespass and intrusion upon seclusion and written in general terms that would, for the most part, apply equally to anyone (California Civil Code Section 1708.8).

Question 2.C: What restrictions and limitations on private data collection by corporations exist?

Consumer privacy laws in the United States are notoriously sector and activity specific. Thus, certain categories of information (financial, health) are subject to specific rules whereas some areas (online advertising) are subject only to the Federal Trade Commission's mandate to police against unfair or deceptive practice. Moreover, the laws in place tend not to restrict collection as such, but rather require notice to the consumer, adequate data security, and so forth. Corporations no less than individuals are still subject to the common law tort of intrusion upon seclusion, wherein the defendant intentionally invades the reasonable expectation of privacy of another through an outrageous conduct.

Question 2.D: What recourse would private citizens have if they feel their privacy rights have been violated by the press, private citizens, or companies using drones?

The opportunities for redress vary by jurisdiction. In many places, citizens may bring suit under one the four common law torts: intrusion upon seclusion, publication of privacy fact, false light, and publicity. Some states have codified these torts and even provided for damages—which can otherwise be a difficult hurdle for a plaintiff to surmount.

Question 3: Is the FAA the best agency for authorizing the domestic use of drones?

I would say that the FAA is a perfectly adequate authority, in the short term, to deal with the privacy issues drones present. The agency's charge from Congress, as I understand it, is to create a comprehensive plan to integrate drones into domestic airspace. I believe successful integration will entail addressing all legitimate citizen discomfort with the technology.

According to a 2012 Government Accountability Office report, one or more FAA officials believe privacy falls outside of the FAA's mission to promote aircraft safety. I respectfully disagree. Agency missions evolve, and other agencies have had no trouble dealing with ancillary factors such as privacy. For instance, in its examination of

W SCHOOL OF LAW
UNIVERSITY of WASHINGTON

driverless cars, the National Highway Traffic Safety Administration has considered the issues of driver privacy and autonomy. And "Safety" is literally their middle name.

I believe the FAA has since acknowledged its potential role in addressing privacy and I am encouraged that, in recent months, the FAA has reached out to the privacy community to seek input in connection with its selection of drone testing sites. I believe the agency can go further and require COA applicants to develop and adhere to a privacy plan or risk losing their certificate, as the Electronic Privacy Information Center has formally requested.

Thank you again for your insightful questions.

SCHOOL OF LAW
UNIVERSITY of WASHINGTON

QUESTION FROM SENATOR MICHAEL LEE

Questions 1: How would the Supreme Court likely decide a case in which law enforcement obtained evidence from the curtilage of—i.e., the area immediately surrounding—the home using an unmanned aircraft system?

In *Florida v. Riley*, the Supreme Court recognized that the area being observed by helicopter was "within the curtilage of the house." I believe the Court would apply the same logic to a standard flyover using an unmanned aircraft system (UAS). I would make several caveats, however:

First, although homeowners do not own all the rights above and below their property as they once did, they still own those air rights they could reasonably use and enjoy. Accordingly, were the UAS to fly low enough to implicate the owner's property rights, one could readily imagine a court treating the act as a trespass and hence a search for purposes of the Fourth Amendment.

Second, a court could conceivably treat peering into a home through a window differently than peering into a greenhouse through a missing tile. A court might apply the reasoning of *Kyllo v. United States*, the thermal imaging case, on the theory that UAS are "sense enhancing technology" not (yet) in public use. Even before *Kyllo*, cases such as *United States v. Taborda*, in the U.S. Court of Appeals for the Second Circuit, held that the use of telescope to look into a dwelling constituted a search.

In short, I believe that the use of a UAS to gather evidence within the area immediately surrounding a home from a reasonable distance would not trigger the Fourth Amendment under current precedent, but could readily imagine facts that would make for a harder case.

Thank you for your great question.

University of Washington School of Law

Senate Committee on the Judiciary

Hearing on "The Future of Drones in America: Law Enforcement and Privacy Considerations"

Questions for the Record

From Ranking Member Charles E. Grassley

Questions for Benjamin Miller

(1) Urban versus Rural Environments

Drone technology can provide valuable assistance to police officers in remote areas where it is hard to reach and inaccessible because of proximity or terrain.

- What type of assistance would drone technology offer police officers in cities or a more urban environment? Unmanned aircraft systems offer much of the same valuable assistance to police officers in urban areas as they do in remote areas. Given the advantages of flight, variables on the ground have minor influence on the outcomes of this equation. In both environments, UAS provide for the opportunity to see from a different vantage point, a 'higher ground' perspective if you will. Whether the device is being used for a search and rescue mission in eastern Montana or a traffic accident investigation in downtown Los Angeles, the assistance is provided from an elevated position.

- Are drones currently being used by law enforcement in urban areas? If yes, what types of drones and drone technology are used in urban areas? Including the Mesa County Sheriff's Office, we are aware of four law enforcement agency operational Certificates of Authorization for the use of UAS. They are U.S. Customs and Border Protection, Grand Forks County (ND) Sheriff's Office, and Arlington (TX) Police Department. The Airborne Law Enforcement Association (ALEA) does not collect data that would answer whether or not these devices are being utilized in urban areas. As such, we would suggest contacting the Federal Aviation Administratation and/or the agencies directly.

- Aside from the use of drones in protecting the Nation's borders, are you aware of any Federal law enforcement agency utilizing drone technology for surveillance or other activity? ALEA does not collect data that would answer this question. We would suggest contacting the Federal Aviation Administratation and/or the agencies directly.

WRITTEN QUESTIONS FROM SENATOR LEE

"The Future of Drones in America: Law Enforcement and Privacy Considerations"
Wednesday, March 20, 2013

Benjamin Miller (Unmanned Aircraft Program Manager, Mesa County Sheriff's Office & Representative of the Airborne Law Enforcement Association)

1. In your testimony, you state that you support the warrant requirement for situations in which persons have reasonable expectations of privacy, but that you would be opposed to restrictions on the use of UAS where such expectations of privacy are absent. This makes it very important that we properly define what constitutes a reasonable expectation of privacy. I know this term has been the subject of many Supreme Court decisions and much has been said in the law on the topic.

2. How you would go about determining when a person has a reasonable expectation of privacy?
   Our process includes the assumption that the fourth amendment applies in every case. We then determine if an already recognized exemption is present. The U.S. Supreme court, throughout the course of this country's history, has established (13) exceptions to the warrant requirement for conducting searches. The exceptions are as follows:

Exigent circumstances	Open fields
Stop and frisk	Abandoned property
Incident to arrest	Consent
Custodial searches	Administrative
Plain view	Probation search
Vehicle	Protective sweep
Border search	

3. In your testimony today, you have noted several legitimate uses of UAS. For example, you note that UAS were used to take pictures of a fire and to help find a missing woman.

   Am I right in concluding that none of your examples implicate the types of privacy concerns that some of us are concerned about, namely the use of UAS to obtain evidence in a criminal proceeding, intrude upon personal privacy, or gather personal data on individuals?

   Not necessarily. In fact, in the church fire example, this was a suspected arson case. No charges have been brought against anyone at this time. But, had charges been filed, these photos would have been deemed evidence and submitted as such. In this case, the flight was not a search and thus no warrant was necessary. It should be noted however, that in the four years that my agency has used unmanned aircraft, we've seen the predominance of use fall under non-criminal operations such as search and rescue.

4. If the beneficial use of UAS you have mentioned do not implicate such concerns, would you support a strict requirement that warrants be obtained for those uses of UAS by law enforcement that implicate these concerns?

As you know, the Fourth Amendment requires a warrant for a search or seizure. When the use of unmanned aircraft has been determined to be a search, under the fourth amendment, a warrant is already required. A duplicative piece of legislation may require further steps that hinder the use of unmanned aircraft for public safety users in operations that are not considered searches under the Fourth Amendment and could unnecessarily add obstacles to saving lives. We feel it would be much more constructive to pursue regulation that addresses how sensitive information can be stored, used and deleted.

Senate Committee on the Judiciary

Hearing on "The Future of Drones in America: Law Enforcement and Privacy Considerations"

Questions for the Record

From Ranking Member Charles E. Grassley

Questions for Amie Stepanovich:

(1) Fourth Amendment Considerations

At the hearing, I asked a number of questions about the application of the Fourth Amendment to the use of unmanned aerial vehicles by law enforcement. I appreciate the answers you provided, but would like to follow-up on a couple of those matters in light of the recent decision by the Supreme Court in *Florida v. Jardines*. In *Jardines*, the Court held, 5-4, that the use of a drug sniffing dog at the front door of a private residence where law enforcement suspect illegal drugs are being grown constitutes a search under the Fourth Amendment.

This decision was based upon the common law notion of trespass extending the Court's reasoning from the 2011 decision in *United States v. Jones*. The majority opinion authored by Justice Scalia reasoned that it was unnecessary to address whether the use of the dog sniff violated the individual's reasonable expectation of privacy, because the trespass onto private property implicated the Fourth Amendment regardless of whether the trespass invades an individual's reasonable expectation of privacy.

- **The use of trespass doctrine to examine the application of the Fourth Amendment to law enforcement activity has implications for the use of drones. Do you believe that the reasoning in both *Jones* and *Jardines* change any of the analysis for reviewing aerial surveillance by unmanned systems under the Fourth Amendment? If so, please describe. If not, why not?**

    In the recent cases of *United States v. Jones*, 132 S. Ct. 945 (2012), and *Florida v. Jardines*, 133 S. Ct. ___ (2013), the Court held that certain law enforcement behavior violated the Fourth Amendment. The majority opinions in both cases focused on the physical intrusion of law enforcement onto private property.
    In both cases, Justice Scalia wrote a majority opinion that made clear that the trespass test was a standard to provide baseline privacy protections, and was not intended to overrule or otherwise change *Katz's* "reasonable expectation of privacy" test. Justice Sotomayor agreed with Scalia in a concurrence in *Jones*, referring to the trespass standard as an "irreducible minimum" of Fourth Amendment protection. Justice Scalia set out a two-part test, first asking if the intrusion violated a constitutionally-protected area (such as the curtilage of the house), and, if so, whether the physical intrusion was unlicensed. In *Jardines*, Scalia noted, "in permitting, for example, visual observation of the home from

'public navigable airspace,' we were careful to note that it was done 'in a physically nonintrusive manner.'"

Drones carry surveillance technology that makes it unnecessary to cross personal property lines in order to obtain sensitive, personal information about an individual, family, group, or organization. Drones are capable of hovering in an area adjacent to the property for prolonged periods of time while collecting vast amounts of personal information. The majority holdings in *Jones* and *Jardines* do not change the test for determining whether the use of drone technology that has not trespassed on private property violates a "reasonable expectation of privacy." Justice Kagan's concurrence in *Jardines* wrote, "where . . . the Government uses a device that is not in general public use, to explore details of the home that would previously have been unknowable without physical intrusion, the surveillance is a 'search' and is presumptively unreasonable without a warrant." But the greater insight of Justice Kagan's concurrence, which was joined by Justice Ginsburg and Justice Sotomayor, is that privacy intrusions can raise concerns under both the trespass doctrine and the *Katz* reasonable expectation of privacy doctrine. This is particularly true, she observed, where the surveillance that takes place is of the home: it is both the trespass onto private property as well as the intrusion into private life that is significant.

The law should clarify in what circumstances a drone has physically invaded or "trespassed" into a constitutionally protected area. Congress could, for example, codify the current standard of up to 400 feet above private property as a minimum basis for a protected area. In addition, comprehensive legislation could preserve current expectations of privacy against increased surveillance, including unregulated data collection and storage.

- **Physical surveillance is difficult and expensive given manpower constraints. Drones can conduct surveillance for hours on end with low cost and little effort. Given the length of time drones can stay on a target, and the low burden on law enforcement, does that change the Fourth Amendment calculus? If so, please explain.**

Practical barriers to surveillance are being reduced by the development of new and inexpensive technologies. The affordability and ease of drone operations will enable increased surveillance unless statutory protections are enacted.

In *United States v. Jones*, the Supreme Court unanimously found that the warrantless attachment and use of a GPS device to a suspect's car for the purpose of monitoring the suspect's movements for a one-month period was a violation of the Fourth Amendment.

The majority opinion in *Jones* rested on a physical trespass rationale. However, a group of four Justices joined Justice Alito's concurring opinion holding that the long-term GPS monitoring also violated a reasonable expectation of privacy. Justice Sotomayor joined the majority opinion, but also wrote in concurrence to note that she agreed with Justice Alito's reasonable expectation of privacy analysis. These concurring opinions created shadow majority in the Jones decision. Justice Alito's opinion held that "the use of longer term GPS monitoring in investigations of most offenses impinges on expectations of privacy," and even though he does not indicate precisely where the line between "short-term" and "long-term" monitoring lies, "the line was surely crossed before the 4-week mark."

Justice Sotomayor agreed with Justice Alito's conclusion that "at the very least, 'longer term GPS monitoring in investigations of most offenses impinges on expectations of privacy.'" Justice Sotomayor noted, "cases involving even short-term monitoring . . . require particular attention" because the "Government can store such records and efficiently mine them for information years into the future." Justice Sotomayor focused on aspects of GPS tracking that also apply to drone technology, namely that it "is cheap . . . proceeds surreptitiously, [and] it evades the ordinary checks that constrain abusive law enforcement practices: 'limited police resources and community hostility.'" Generally, the Court's analysis suggests that in the absence of a legal standard enacted by Congress, drone surveillance will proliferate over time.

- **Does the addition of technology, such as facial recognition, biometric recognition, and thermal imaging equipment, affect whether there is a reasonable expectation of privacy under the Fourth Amendment? If so, please explain.**

Drones already carry infrared cameras, heat sensors, GPS, sensors that detect movement, and automated license plate readers. In the near future, government and corporate actors may attempt to outfit drones with facial recognition technology, Stingray cell-site simulators, and electronic frisking scanners.

The use of this technology to conduct surveillance of activities within the home (e.g. thermal imaging) should trigger Fourth Amendment protections. In *Kyllo v. United States*, 533 U.S. 72 (2001), and, more recently, in Justice Kagan's concurring opinion in *Florida v. Jardines*, the Court indicated that "where [a] device is not in general public use, training it on a home violates our minimal expectation of privacy." Absent Congressional action to preserve current expectations of privacy, the availability and proliferation of surveillance technology may degrade the current standards of privacy protection against surveillance in and around the home.

The curtilage, or the area directly surrounding the home, enjoys special Fourth Amendment protections similar to the home itself *United States v. Hester*, 365 U.S. 57 (1924). In *Florida v. Jardines*, the Court held that the curtilage "is part of the home itself for Fourth Amendment purposes." However, the Court has previous allowed warrantless law enforcement surveillance of the curtilage from the vantage point of a fixed-wing manned aircraft flying over the home within the public airspace. *Florida v. Riley*, 488 U.S. 445 (1989), *see also California v Ciraolo*, 476 U.S. 207 (1986). By contrast, at least one Circuit Court has held that long-term fixed-camera surveillance of curtilage violated the Fourth Amendment *United States v. Anderson-Bagshaw*, 2012 WL 6600331 (2012). Courts will continue to struggle with the question of when surveillance of the curtilage using advanced technology constitutes a Fourth Amendment search.

As Justice Sotomayor's concurring opinion in *Jones* explained, extended surveillance, such as that made possible by advanced technologies, can generate "a wealth of data" about a person and reveal intimate details of their life that would not otherwise be public. Because of this risk to privacy, Congress should set defined limits on the warrantless use of these technologies, even in public spaces.

(2) First Amendment Considerations

The use of drones by private entities, such as the news media, to gather information on individuals and organizations is fast becoming a reality. Government regulation of private drone use is likely to be a new battleground under First Amendment. Even now, states legislators are proposing new laws to severely curtail the use of drones by private persons and entities. For example, a new bill proposed in California would prevent people or entities not affiliated with the government from using unmanned aircraft "for the purpose of surveillance of another person without that person's consent.

The First Amendment protects the freedom of the press, subject to reasonable restrictions. Drone technology could potentially offer the press a powerful tool in terms of surveillance.

- **Does the First Amendment prohibit Congress from restricting use of drone technology by the press?**

    Drones do not enjoy more Constitutional protection than other technologies or methods for newsgathering or documentation. As with all forms of expression, content-based restrictions on drones would be unconstitutional under the First Amendment. Laws such as the Video Voyeurism Protection Act and state paparazzi laws are currently in force that restrict image collection in certain, limited situations.

- **What reasonable restrictions could Congress consider placing on the use of drone technology by the press?**

    Over private property, laws could define the parameters under which a drone would commit a trespass, violate a reasonable expectation of privacy, or intrude upon an individual's right of enjoyment of his or her property. Non-content based restrictions on the use of drones may be permissible. For example, Congress could clarify the current standard by defining individual property ownership of the airspace up to 400 feet and codify current expectations of privacy against increased surveillance.

    However, even non-content based restrictions on the use of drones by individuals should be carefully considered. Drones may be powerful tools for journalism in many instances. For instance, in holding public officials accountable in the performance of their official duties or reporting on weather-related events, such as hurricanes or earthquakes.

- **With regard to commercial applications, we have heard concerns about the increased use of private data collected by companies for advertising or other business purposes. What restrictions and limitations on private data collection by corporations exist?**

    There is not a comprehensive privacy law in the United States to restrict the collection or use of personal information by commercial entities. A patchwork of sector-specific laws include protections for privacy, such as the Gramm-Leach-Bliley Act and the Fair Credit Reporting Act. In addition, the Federal Trade Commission investigates "unlawful or deceptive" trade practices by industry, including those involving corporate privacy practices.

    The Electronic Communications Privacy Act ("ECPA") restricts the interception of wire, oral, or electronic communications. In 2012, the U.S. Department of Justice refused to file charges against Google, Inc. after the company had intercepted Wi-Fi data with Wi-Fi receivers concealed in the Company's Street View vehicles. Following independent investigations, Google conceded that it gathered MAC addresses (the unique device ID for Wi-Fi hotposts) and network SSIDs (the user-assigned network ID name) that it stored along with location information for private wireless networks. Google also admits that it intercepted and stored Wi-Fi transmission data, which included email passwords and email content. Congress should clarify that such practices are impermissible.

- **What recourse would private citizens have if they feel that their privacy rights have been violated by the press, or by other private citizens or companies utilizing drones?**

    Absent Congressional action to create private right of action, individuals have limited recourse available to them against a private citizen or company who operates a drone in a way to violates their privacy or civil liberties. While some relief may be available under the U.S. common law for torts or pursuant to state laws, these protections are inconsistent and insufficient to address the unique aspects of surveillance made possible by drones. When the drone operator can be identified, a criminal action may be maintained in some states in the more egregious circumstances, such as stalking. This, however, also becomes an issue since drones may be operated in a manner to make identification of the operator difficult, and there are currently no public licensing requirements.

(3) Regulation of Unmanned Aerial Vehicles by the Federal Aviation Administration (FAA)

The Federal Aviation Administration (FAA) is currently the lead federal agency in approving the use of drones in the public airspace. Law enforcement agencies, civilian agencies, and individuals must apply with the FAA for a permit to authorize domestic drones.

- **In your opinion, is the FAA the best agency for authorizing the domestic use of drones? If not, what additional agencies should be involved?**

The FAA is required to "promote safe flight of civil aircraft." The FAA Modernization and Reform Act requires the FAA to, within a certain amount of time, "develop a comprehensive plan" to implement drones into civil commerce. Before May 14, 2012 the FAA must "simply the process" by which government entities operate drones in the national airspace. This authority places the FAA into the best position to assess many of the privacy problems associated with the highly intrusive nature of drone aircraft, and the ability of operators to gain access to private areas and to track individuals over large distances.

In addition, to the extent that the Department of Homeland Security, as well as other agencies that choose to operate drones, are responsible for greater aerial surveillance of individuals within the United States, we believe that the Agency should also develop appropriate regulations to safeguard privacy. Congress should require all agencies choosing to own and operate drones to promulgate, subject to the public notice and comment provisions of the Administrative Procedure Act (5 U.S.C. § 553), rules and standards for the protection of individual privacy and civil liberties.

Senate Committee on the Judiciary
Hearing on "The Future of Drones in America: Law Enforcement and Privacy Considerations"
Questions for the Record
From Ranking Member Charles E. Grassley

Questions for Michael Toscano:

(1) Addition of Technology to Unmanned Aerial Platforms

News reports have identified a wide range of technology that can be used with drones. For example, we have heard reports about thermal imaging equipment, high resolution cameras, sound recording devices, facial recognition tools, and biometric recognition tools.

- What technology is currently being used on drones to help law enforcement in criminal investigations?
- What technology is currently available to help farmers and those involved in agriculture?
- What types of limitations should Congress consider which would protect the privacy rights of law abiding citizens without stifling innovation in the private sector?

Answer from Michael Toscano:

What technology is currently being used on drones to help law enforcement in criminal investigations?

Due to size and weight constraints, especially on small UAS, the cameras or sensors on a UAS are significantly less advanced than cameras or sensors on manned aircraft, including police helicopters. During the hearing, Ben Miller with the Mesa County Sheriff's Office testified that that his small rotorcraft UAS is equipped with "a low cost point and click camera" that can be bought at Wal-Mart.

Currently, there are fewer than five law enforcement agencies that have permission from the FAA to fly for operational missions. Those that do have approval are usually limited to flying during the daytime, less than 400 feet in altitude, and within visual line of sight, all of which are required for safety reasons. Even with these limitations, law enforcement and public safety agencies still want to use UAS to get better situational awareness, and the best way to do that is from above. Here are a few ways UAS can help in public safety:

- **Supporting law enforcement.** Like other first responders, law enforcement officers and border patrol agents work in dangerous environments. UAS can be invaluable in aiding search and rescue missions, pursuing a fugitive loose in a neighborhood or offer a critical vantage point when responding to a hostage situation. In February 2013, a UAS was used by law enforcement responding to a hostage situation in Alabama.

    UAS also help law enforcement agencies cut costs. Operating manned police helicopters can cost between $200 and $400 per hour, while operating an unmanned aircraft can cost as low as $25 to $75 per hour. The purchase price of a UAS can also be significantly less than a manned aircraft. A small UAS can cost less than $50,000, which is about the price of a patrol car with standard police gear.

- **Fighting fires safely and strategically.** Firefighters and other first responders do their jobs in incredibly dangerous environments. UAS can minimize the risks they face, while helping them to act faster and with the best information available to save lives. Able to fly through smoke-filled skies too dangerous for manned flights, UAS give firefighters the ability to better understand the circumstances they are facing, such as the size and scope of a wildfire or hotspots in a burning building, before putting a firefighter in harm's way.

  In 2008, NASA assisted the state of California in fighting wildfires with the use of a UAS. The information about the fires was transmitted to command centers within minutes, and then distributed into the field giving firefighters crucial situational awareness. Throughout the operation, NASA pilots operating the UAS were in close communication with the FAA to ensure its safe separation from other aircraft.

- **Improving search and rescue.** UAS can reach higher vantage points and survey a large search grid for a missing child, acres of land consumed by wild fires or vast expanses of water where a boat might be adrift. Bad weather and difficult terrain can prolong search and rescue efforts, lowering chances for survival while raising the financial cost. However, UAS make searching for lost hikers and missing persons cheaper, faster and safer than using manned helicopters.

- **Responding to disasters.** UAS can enter hazardous spaces too dangerous, difficult or costly for humans to enter. UAS have been used to survey flooding in the upper Midwest to assess damage and provide responders and engineers with live video and radar. NASA recently flew UAS into a Costa Rican volcano's plume – a mission that could destroy a manned aircraft's engines. UAS were also used in Japan following the 2011 earthquake-induced tsunami, which damaged the nuclear facility in Fukushima. With leaking radiation making it impossible for emergency responders to approach the facility's reactors, a UAS was used to fly over the damaged facility and use advanced sensors to help responders gain situational awareness.

What technology is currently available to help farmers and those involved in agriculture?

Currently, the FAA does not allow for commercial use of UAS, including for agriculture. The FAA's UAS policy requires operators who wish to fly for civil use obtain an airworthiness certificate the same as any other type of aircraft. However, the FAA is currently only issuing special airworthiness certificates in the experimental category. Experimental certificates are issued with accompanying operational limitations, which only allow them to be flown for research and development, marketing surveys, or crew training. Until the FAA writes the safety rules, UAS will not be allowed to fly for commercial purposes. Congress directed the FAA to implement those safety rules by October 2015.

However, as was stated in my testimony, an economic report on UAS recently released by my organization projects that agriculture will make up 80 percent of the potential commercial UAS market, for crop surveys and precision applications. A variety of remote sensors are being used to scan plants for health problems, record growth rates and hydration, and locate disease outbreaks. Precision application, a practice especially useful for crop farmers and horticulturists, utilizes effective and efficient spray techniques to more selectively cover plants and fields. This allows farmers to provide only the needed pesticide or nutrient to each plant, reducing the total amount sprayed, and thus saving money and reducing environmental impacts.

While the farmers in the U.S. are still prohibited from using UAS, farmers in Japan have been taking advantage of the technology for the past two decades. According to manufacturer Yamaha, in 2011, there more than 2,300 unmanned helicopters registered in Japan performing 90 percent of the nation's crop spraying. The advantages afforded by using UAS in agriculture include improved operational efficiency, zero soil compaction, zero crop damage, superior spray deposition, reduced applicator exposure to chemicals and increased operator safety.

What types of limitations should Congress consider which would protect the privacy rights of law abiding citizens without stifling innovation in the private sector?

AUVSI supports the development and advancement of UAS technology in a safe and responsible manner, while respecting existing privacy laws and ensuring transparency and accountability. To help safeguard Americans' right to privacy, **AUVSI supports**:

- The registration of unmanned aircraft and pilots with the Federal Aviation Administration (FAA).
- The enforcement of established law and policy, governing the collection, use, storage, sharing and deletion of data, regardless of how it is collected.
    - These policies should be available for public review.
    - The policies should outline strict accountability for unauthorized use.
- The International Association of Chiefs of Police recommended guidelines for UAS operations and their recommendations on data collection, which have been adopted by the Airborne Law Enforcement Association and others.
- The 4th Amendment's requirement that the government obtain a search warrant before intruding upon someone's reasonable expectation of privacy.
- Holding accountable any individual who misuses any technology to unlawfully violate someone's privacy through illegal surveillance. UAS manufacturers should not be held responsible for improper or illegal use of unmanned aircraft systems.

This issue should focus on the extent to which the government can collect, use and store personal data – which is why transparency and accountability are key. Instead of focusing on how the government collects information, AUVSI supports an open debate on the government's right to collect, use, store, share, and delete personal data.

When considering drafting federal legislation aimed at protecting privacy, Congress must be careful to not stifle this new industry before it is allowed to even take off. In a recent article entitled, *Observations from Above: Unmanned Aircraft Systems and Privacy*, 36 Harvard Journal of Law and Public Policy 457-517 (2013), John Villasenor, a UCLA professor and Brookings Institution Nonresident Senior Fellow, concluded,

> When considering potential new statutory UAS privacy protections, it is helpful to keep in mind what has occurred with the Internet and mobile telephones, two technologies that are associated with privacy threats that are in some respects much more significant than those that will arise from unmanned aircraft. Both the Internet and mobile phones grew as fast as their underlying technologies enabled. As a result, the public and legislative dialogue regarding how best to address the privacy issues they raise has been conducted with a strong appreciation of their benefits. By contrast, while the privacy concerns associated with domestic UAS are real and deserving of attention, they are getting significant focus long before the potential benefits of the technology are widely recognized.

With this in mind, it is important to note that although the United States is currently the world leader in UAS technology, the rest of the world is working hard to catch up. In fact, many countries, such as Canada, Australia, Germany, England, and others, allow for routine small UAS flights for commercial purposes, including agriculture, infrastructure monitoring, photography, and public safety. This is a competitiveness issue, and it would be unfortunate for the United States to stifle this new aerospace industry.

AUVSI contends that the FAA is the wrong agency to oversee UAS-related privacy issues. The FAA should focus on its stated mission, which is to provide the safest, most efficient aerospace systems in the world. The FAA's criteria for permitting access to the airspace should solely be based on safety.

Other federal agencies with expertise dealing with privacy issues, such as the U.S. Department of Justice, the Department of Homeland Security, as well as the judicial system, could address privacy.

AUVSI believes information gathered by a UAS should be treated no differently than information gathered by a manned aircraft, or any other electronic means. Any new legislation or regulation addressing privacy should be technology neutral.

AUVSI looks forward to continuing to work with you, the Senate Judiciary Committee, and the Congress as this technology matures and begins to be used to do tasks that are currently to dangerous, difficult, dull, or expensive for manned aircraft.

WRITTEN QUESTIONS FROM SENATOR LEE

"The Future of Drones in America: Law Enforcement and Privacy Considerations"
Wednesday, March 20, 2013

Michael Toscano (CEO of Association for Unmanned Vehicle Systems International)

1. In your testimony, you stated that there currently is a "robust legal framework" with respect to privacy and the use of Unmanned Aircraft Systems or UAS. With respect to constitutional violations of privacy, the Supreme Court has never spoken directly to the issue of the application of the Fourth Amendment to UAS. And it seems somewhat unclear how the Court would apply precedents such as *Kyllo* and *Jones* to a case in which evidence was obtained using UAS.

    a. What legal framework is currently in place with respect to privacy and the use of UAS and do you think that framework is adequate?

2. There has been some discussion today of the role of the FAA in imposing restrictions on the use of UAS to protect privacy. It is my understanding that the FAA, in implementing its statutory duty to integrate UAS into national airspace, is considering privacy policies.

    a. Do you support the FAA making privacy protection an integral part of their UAS licensing scheme, and if so, what are some of the more important considerations they should include in their analysis?

Response from Michael Toscano

1. Senator Lee, you are correct that there are currently no U.S. Supreme Court cases directly addressing Constitutional privacy issues related to evidence gathered from an unmanned aircraft system (UAS), primarily because this technology is new and only a handful of law enforcement agencies have permission to fly a UAS.

    However, the Supreme Court has reviewed the implications of technology and aerial surveillance for the past several decades, and AUVSI believes these cases provide valuable precedent in which to consider UAS. It is important to recognize upfront that although the vehicle may be different, the system it is carrying, usually a camera or sensor, are often the same used on manned aircraft. Simply removing the pilot from the aircraft does not change the fact that there is always a human responsible for the flight.

    As John Villasenor stated in a recent article, *Observations from Above: Unmanned Aircraft Systems and Privacy*, (36 Harvard Journal of Law and Public Policy 457-517 (2013)) "a careful examination of Supreme Court privacy jurisprudence suggests that the Constitution will provide a much stronger measure of protection against government UAS privacy abuses than is widely appreciated. The Fourth Amendment has served us well since its ratification in 1791, and there is no reason to suspect it will be unable to do so in a world where unmanned aircraft are widely used. In addition, there are substantial statutory and common law protections that will limit the ability of non-government entities to violate privacy using manned aircraft."

As you know, the Fourth Amendment of the U.S. Constitution prohibits unreasonable searches and seizures and requires search warrants to be based upon probable cause. Although I am not a lawyer, or a Constitutional expert, below are some U.S. Supreme Court cases I believe are relevant to the discussion of the government's use aircraft and technology for surveillance. In talking with law enforcement, they are comfortable with the rules established by the Court, and they are confident they can utilize UAS technology in full compliance with them.

In *Katz v. United States* (1967), the Supreme Court found it unconstitutional to place an eavesdropping device on a closed public phone booth saying, the "Fourth Amendment search occurs when the government violates a subjective expectation of privacy that society recognizes as reasonable". "These considerations do not vanish when the search in question is transferred from the setting of a home, an office, or a hotel room to that of a telephone booth." "Wherever a man may be, he is entitled to know that he will remain free from unreasonable searches and seizures." This case extended an individual's right to privacy outside of their home.

In *California v. Ciraolo* (1986), the Court created the "reasonable expectation of privacy" test, which the Court found the police did not violate when it flew a small manned airplane over private property and photographed marijuana growing in a backyard (within the curtilage of the defendants home). That observation and the photographs taken were used to secure a search warrant to seize the marijuana. The Court found, "the Fourth Amendment protection of the home has never been extended to require law enforcement officers to shield their eyes when passing by a home on public thoroughfares." The Court considered "public navigable airspace" a thoroughfare and found it permissible for the police to fly anywhere the general public has the right to fly.

In *Dow Chemical Company v. United States* (1986), which was decided on the same day as *California v. Ciraolo*, the Court found it permissible for the Environmental Protection Agency to fly a manned aircraft over a business and take detailed pictures from a sophisticated mapping camera, ruling, "The taking of aerial photographs of an industrial plant complex from navigable airspace is not a search prohibited by the Fourth Amendment."

In *Florida v. Riley* (1989), the Court found it permissible for the police to fly a manned helicopter 400 feet above a greenhouse, which was located behind a home, and use observations made by looking through missing window panels to secure a warrant to seize the marijuana being grown inside. The Court affirmed its reasoning in *Ciraolo*, saying, "Any member of the public could legally have been flying over Riley's property in a helicopter at the altitude of 400 feet and could have observed Riley's greenhouse. The police officer did no more."

In *Kyllo v. United States* (2001), the Court held that the use of a thermal imaging device from a public vantage point to monitor the radiation of heat from a person's home was a search within the meaning of the Fourth Amendment and thus required a search warrant. The Court found that allowing the government to collect information emanating from a house would put people "at the mercy of advancing technology – including imaging technology that could discern all human activity in the home."

Although the Court discussed at length whether or not a "device is in general public use", the fact remains that when people have a Constitutional right to privacy, the police need a warrant to conduct a search, regardless of the technology being used. If it is unconstitutional for the police to use a handheld thermal imaging device from their police car on a public street, it will also be unconstitutional for the police to use a thermal imaging device to look at a house from a manned aircraft, or a UAS, absent a warrant.

Recently, the Court in *United States v. Jones* (2012) found the police violated the Fourth Amendment on trespassing grounds by sticking a global positioning system tracker on a car to monitor a person's whereabouts for an extended period of time. The Court acknowledged that extended electronic surveillance without a physical trespass *may* violate the Fourth Amendment; however, the Court declined to rule on those grounds.

Earlier this year, the Court once again found an unreasonable trespass when it ruled in *Florida v. Jardines* (2013) that the police cannot bring a drug-sniffing dog on your front porch to inspect for drugs without a warrant.

Clearly, there are lots of ways to track someone's whereabouts, or monitor activities electronically, and it would not be surprising if someday the Court takes up a case, similar to *Kyllo*, where they address an individual's right to privacy, without ruling on trespass grounds. However, given that cases are fact specific, it is too early to tell how the Court will rule on electronic surveillance without a trespass.

If Congress wants to consider legislation addressing UAS privacy issues, it should do so in a technologically-neutral way. Ultimately, the issue is about data. Does the government have the right to collect and use data it gathers by any sort of means against you?

As you know, the government uses a lot of tools that can collect information on us; however, they do not routinely violate our privacy rights because they have policies and procedures in place. The best way to ensure government does not abuse its power is to ensure transparency and accountability. In the event the police use technology improperly, the judicial system is there to hold the government in check. Evidence gathered improperly is not allowed to be used. To echo John Villasenor's comments, our current system has served us well for over 222 years, and there is no reason to think we cannot handle this new technology.

AUVSI does not believe the FAA is the appropriate agency to govern the privacy implications of UAS operations. The FAA should focus on its stated mission, which is to provide the safest, most efficient aerospace systems in the world.

Other federal agencies with expertise dealing with privacy issues, such as the U.S. Department of Justice, the Department of Homeland Security, as well as the judicial system, could address privacy. The FAA's criteria for permitting access to the airspace should solely be based on safety.

AUVSI believes information gathered by a UAS should be treated no differently than information gathered by a manned aircraft, or any other electronic means, as was discussed above in my answer to your first question. Any new legislation or regulation addressing privacy should be technology neutral.

2. You are correct to point out that the FAA is currently soliciting public comments on how to address privacy issues related to the establishment of six UAS test sites around the country, which Congress called for in the FAA Modernization and Reform Act (Public Law 112-95). However, nowhere in the FAA law did Congress direct the FAA to regulate UAS based on privacy issues.

The FAA intends to use the Congressionally-mandated UAS test sites to collect valuable safety data, which will help it create safety rules. However, in response to privacy concerns raised by the public and some in Congress, the FAA has published a notice of availability and request for comments in the Federal Register (Docket No. FAA-2013-0061). In addition to collecting safety data, the UAS test sites will also help educate the public about UAS and provide best practices for community engagement, transparency, and accountability.

Below are the UAS test site privacy policy requirements the FAA is currently soliciting public comment on:

(1) The Site Operator must ensure that there are privacy policies governing all activities conducted under the OTA [Other Transaction Agreement], including the operation and relevant activities of the UASs authorized by the Site Operator. Such privacy policies must be available publically, and the Site Operator must have a mechanism to receive and consider comments on its privacy policies. In addition, these policies should be informed by Fair Information Practice Principles. The privacy policies should be updated as necessary to remain operationally current and effective. The Site Operator must ensure the requirements of this paragraph are applied to all operations conducted under the OTA.

(2) The Site Operator and its team members are required to operate in accordance with Federal, state, and other laws regarding the protection of an individual's right to privacy. Should criminal or civil charges be filed by the U.S. Department of Justice or a state's law enforcement authority over a potential violation of such laws, the FAA may take

appropriate action, including suspending or modifying the relevant operational authority (e.g., Certificate of Operation, or OTA), until the proceedings are completed. If the proceedings demonstrate the operation was in violation of the law, the FAA may terminate the relevant operational authority.

(3) If over the lifetime of this Agreement, any legislation or regulation, which may have an impact on UAS or to the privacy interests of entities affected by any operation of any UAS operating at the Test Site, is enacted or otherwise effectuated, such legislation or regulation will be applicable to the OTA, and the FAA may update or amend the OTA to reflect these changes.

(4) Transmission of data from the Site Operator to the FAA or its designee must only include those data listed in Appendix B to the OTA. (Appendix B to the OTA is available as part of the SIR [Screening Information Request] at *http://faaco.faa.gov*.)

The FAA anticipates that test site operator privacy practices as discussed in their privacy policies will help inform the dialogue among policymakers, privacy advocates, and the industry regarding broader questions concerning the use of UAS technologies. The privacy requirements proposed here are specifically designed for the operation of the UAS Test Sites. They are not intended to pre-determine the long-term policy and regulatory framework under which commercial UASs would operate. Rather, they aim to assure maximum transparency of privacy policies associated with UAS test site operations in order to engage all stakeholders in discussion about which privacy issues are raised by UAS operations and how law, public policy, and the industry practices should respond to those issues in the long run.

AUVSI supports the development and advancement of UAS technology in a safe and responsible manner, while respecting existing privacy laws and ensuring transparency and accountability. AUVSI supports the registration of unmanned aircraft and pilots with the FAA, much like they do for manned aircraft. AUVSI supports the creation and enforcement of policies governing the collection, use, storage, sharing, and deletion of data, regardless of how it is collected. Those policies should be available for public review, and they should outline strict accountability for unauthorized use.

Furthermore, AUVSI supports the International Association of Chiefs of Police recommended guidelines for UAS operations and their recommendations on data collection. AUVSI supports the Fourth Amendment's requirement that the government obtain a search warrant whenever someone's reasonable expectation of privacy is violated, and AUVSI supports holding accountable individuals who misuse any technology to violate privacy laws. AUVSI does not condone the use of UAS for illegal surveillance.

As Congress and regulators continue to examine UAS and work towards implementing UAS into the airspace, it is important to tread carefully. Onerous laws or rules, aimed at restricting UAS development and use, will stifle a new industry that has the potential to create 70,000 new jobs and bring over $13 billion in economic growth within the first three years of integration. There should be no doubt, the future of aviation is unmanned, and the United States can remain the global leader in this new competitive field; however, only if this new industry is allowed to grow without undue burdens.

AUVSI looks forward to continuing to work with you, the Senate Judiciary Committee, and the Congress as this technology develops.

SUBMISSIONS FOR THE RECORD

ACLU
AMERICAN CIVIL LIBERTIES UNION

WRITTEN STATEMENT OF
THE AMERICAN CIVIL LIBERTIES UNION

For a Hearing on

"The Future of Drones in America: Law Enforcement and Privacy Considerations"

Submitted to the Senate Judiciary Committee

March 20, 2013

ACLU Washington Legislative Office
Laura W. Murphy, Director
Christopher Calabrese, Legislative Counsel
Jay Stanley, Senior Policy Analyst
Catherine Crump, Staff Attorney

The American Civil Liberties Union (ACLU) submits this statement to the Senate Judiciary Committee on the occasion of its hearing addressing "The Future of Drones in America: Law Enforcement and Privacy Considerations." This statement describes the privacy and civil liberties implications of the domestic use of unmanned surveillance vehicles, also known as drones, and recommends new protections for use of the technology.

I. Introduction

Unmanned aircraft carrying cameras raise the prospect of a significant new avenue for the surveillance of American life. Many Americans are familiar with these aircraft, commonly called drones, because of their use overseas in places like Afghanistan and Yemen. But drones are coming to America. Recently passed legislation requires the Federal Aviation Administration to "develop a comprehensive plan to safely accelerate the integration of civil unmanned aircraft systems into the national airspace system."[1] This new legislation has dramatically accelerated the deployment of drones and pushed this issue to the forefront. Meanwhile, the technology is quickly becoming cheaper and more powerful, interest in deploying drones among police departments is increasing, and our privacy laws are not strong enough to ensure that the new technology will be used responsibly and consistently with constitutional values. In short, the specter of routine aerial surveillance in American life is on the near horizon — a development that would profoundly change the character of public life in the United States.

We need a system of rules to ensure that Americans can enjoy the benefits of this technology without bringing our country a large step closer to a "surveillance society" in which every move is monitored, tracked, recorded, and scrutinized by the authorities. This statement outlines a set of protections that would protect Americans' privacy in the coming world of drones.

Aerial surveillance from manned aircraft has been with us for decades. One of the first aircraft the Wright brothers built was a surveillance aircraft, and it was sold to the U.S. Army. Many common uses of drone aircraft—search and rescue, fighting wildfires, dangerous tactical police operations—are beneficial. In the 1980s the Supreme Court ruled that the Fourth Amendment does not categorically prohibit the government from carrying out warrantless aerial surveillance of private property.

But manned aircraft are expensive to purchase, operate and maintain, and this expense has always imposed a natural limit on the government's aerial surveillance capability. Now that surveillance can be carried out by unmanned aircraft, this natural limit is eroding. The prospect of cheap, small, portable flying video surveillance machines threatens to eradicate existing practical limits on aerial monitoring and allow for pervasive surveillance, police fishing expeditions, and abusive use of these tools in a way that could eventually eliminate the privacy Americans have traditionally enjoyed in their movements and activities. In order to prevent this harmful and invasive outcome, Congress must act.

II. The Technology

---

[1] FAA Modernization and Reform Act of 2012, P.L. 112-95, §332, 126 Stat.11, 73.

There are hundreds of different types of Unmanned Aerial Vehicles (UAVs), as drones are formally known.[2] They can be as large as commercial aircraft or as small as hummingbirds, and include human remotely guided aircraft as well as autonomous, self-guided vehicles. They include:

- **Large fixed-wing aircraft.** The largest UAVs currently in use, such as the Israeli-made Eitan, are about the size of a Boeing 737 jetliner. The Eitan's wingspan is 86 feet, and it can stay aloft for 20 hours and reach an altitude of 40,000 feet.[3] The Predator B drone, which has been used extensively on overseas battlefields as well as on the U.S.-Mexico border, has a wingspan of 66 feet, and it can stay aloft for over 30 hours and reach an altitude of 50,000 feet.[4] In Pakistan and Afghanistan, the U.S. military and CIA deploy Predators and Reapers armed with surveillance capability as well as missiles capable of destroying a moving vehicle from thousands of feet in the air.[5]

- **Small fixed-wing aircraft.** Smaller fixed-wing aircraft are the current favorite for domestic deployment. The Houston police department, for example, recently tested the ScanEagle, made by Boeing subsidiary Insitu.[6] The ScanEagle is 4 ½ feet long with a wingspan of 10 feet, and it can climb to 19,500 feet and stay aloft for more than 24 hours.[7]

- **Backpack craft.** Another class of craft is designed to be carried and operated by a single person. The hand-launched AeroVironment Raven, for example, weighs 4 pounds, has a wingspan of 4.5 feet and a length of 3 feet, can fly up to 14,000 feet and stay aloft for up to 110 minutes. Similar-sized products include a three-foot helicopter called the Draganflyer X6, a one-foot-long, one-pound fixed-wing craft called the AeroVironment Wasp, and a fan-propelled craft called the Honeywell T-Hawk that can "hover and stare." Individual hobbyists have also built a number of drones in this size range.[8]

---

[2] See Wikipedia, "List of unmanned aerial vehicles," at http://en.wikipedia.org/wiki/List_of_unmanned_aerial_vehicles.
[3] "Israel unveils world's largest UAV," Homeland Security Newswire, Feb. 23, 2010, online at http://homelandsecuritynewswire.com/israel-unveils-worlds-largest-uav.
[4] See General Atomics web page on Predator B at http://www.ga-asi.com/products/aircraft/predator_b.php; R.P.G. Collinson, Introduction to Avionic Systems (2011), p. 495
[5] Yochi J. Dreazen, "From Pakistan, With Love: The technology used to monitor the skies over Waziristan is coming to your hometown," National Journal, March 13, 2011, online at http://www.nationaljournal.com/magazine/drones-may-be-coming-to-your-hometown-20110313.
[6] Stephen Dean, "Police line up to use drones on patrol after Houston secret test," Houston Examiner, Jan. 11, 2010, online at http://www.examiner.com/page-one-in-houston/police-line-up-to-use-drones-on-patrol-after-houston-secret-test.
[7] Insitu, ScanEagle brochure, online at http://www.insitu.com/documents/Insitu%20Website/Marketing%20Collateral/ScanEagle%20Folder%20Insert.pdf
[8] AeroVironment brochure, online at http://www.avinc.com/downloads/Raven_Domestic_1210.pdf; AeroVironment web page on the Wasp at http://www.avinc.com/uas/small_uas/wasp/; Carrie Kahn, "It's A Bird! It's A Plane! It's A Drone!" National Public Radio, March 14, 2011, online at http://www.npr.org/2011/03/14/134533552/its-a-bird-its-a-plane-its-a-drone; "Drones on the home front," Washington Post, Jan. 23, 2011, online at http://www.washingtonpost.com/wp-srv/special/nation/drone-gallery/

- **Hummingbirds.** A tiny drone called the Nano Hummingbird was developed for the Pentagon's Defense Advanced Research Projects Agency (DARPA) by AeroVironment. Intended for stealth surveillance, it can fly up to 11 miles per hour and can hover, fly sideways, backwards and forwards, for about 8 minutes. It has a wingspan of 6.5 inches and weighs only 19 grams—less than a single AA battery.[9]

- **Blimps.** Some blimps are envisioned as high-altitude craft, up to 300 feet in diameter, that would compete with satellites, while others would be low-altitude craft that would allow the police to monitor the streets. Supporters say they are more cost-effective than other craft due to their ability to stay aloft for extended periods.[10]

III. Drone Capabilities—Today and in the Future

The aircraft themselves are steadily improving and, as with so many technologies, that is likely to continue. They are becoming smaller. The military and law enforcement are keenly interested in developing small drones, which have the advantages of being versatile, cheap to buy and maintain, and in some cases so small and quiet that they will escape notice.[11] They are also becoming cheaper. The amazing continual decreases in the prices of electronics that have become normal in our time all but guarantee that the surveillance technologies attached to UAVs will become less expensive and yet more powerful—and with mass production, the aircraft that carry those electronics will become inexpensive enough for a police department to fill the skies over a town with them.

Drones are also becoming smarter. Artificial intelligence advances will likely help drones carry out spying missions. Korean researchers, for example, are working to teach robots how to hide from and sneak up upon a subject.[12] They also will have better staying power, with a greater ability to stay aloft for longer periods of time. Mechanisms for increasing time aloft could include solar power, or the use of blimps or gliders.[13]

Although the primary uses of drones so far have been military, even on overseas battlefields their main use is surveillance. The larger drones can be fitted with weapons or other

---

[9] W.J. Hennigan, "It's a bird! It's a spy! It's both," Los Angeles Times, Feb. 17, 2011, online at http://articles.latimes.com/2011/feb/17/business/la-fi-hummingbird-drone-20110217.

[10] On high-altitude blimps see Elliott Minor, "Interest Growing in 'Security' Blimps," Associated Press, April 27, 2004, available online at http://www.rustysforum.com/cgi-bin/domains/com/rustysforum/frc_bb/ultimatebb.cgi?ubb=next_topic&f=1&t=000807&go=older; on low-altitude blimps see e.g. James Nelson, "Utah city may use blimp as anti-crime spy in the sky," Reuters, Jan. 16, 2011, online at http://www.reuters.com/article/2011/01/16/us-crime-blimp-utah-idUSTRE70F1DJ20110116.

[11] W.J. Hennigan, "It's a bird! It's a spy! It's both," Los Angeles Times, Feb. 17, 2011, online at http://articles.latimes.com/2011/feb/17/business/la-fi-hummingbird-drone-20110217.

[12] M. Ryan Calo, "Robots and Privacy," April 2010, online at http://ssrn.com/abstract=1599189.

[13] "Gliders Emerge As Surveillance UAVs," Aviation Week, June 8, 2010, online at http://www.aviationweek.com/aw/generic/story_generic.jsp?topicName=ila_2010&id=news/awx/2010/06/08/awx_0 6_08_2010_p0-232627.xml; James Nelson, "Utah city may use blimp as anti-crime spy in the sky," Reuters, Jan. 16, 2011, online at http://www.reuters.com/article/2011/01/16/us-crime-blimp-utah-idUSTRE70F1DJ20110116; Ned Smith, "Solar-powered UAV can stay aloft 5 years," TechNewsDaily, Sept. 22, 2010, online at http://www.msnbc.msn.com/id/39313306/ns/technology_and_science-tech_and_gadgets/t/solar-powered-uav-can-stay-aloft-years.

heavy payloads, but all of them can carry cameras and other imaging technologies that have developed amazing capabilities in recent years and are likely to become even more capable in the near future.

Except for possibly the very lightest craft, drones can carry the full range of advanced surveillance technologies that have been developed—and are likely to be developed—including:

- **High-power zoom lenses.** UAVs can carry increasingly powerful lenses that allow significant zooming, increasing the chance that individuals will come under scrutiny from faraway aircraft without knowing it. And the density of photo sensors is growing at an exponential pace (in line with Moore's law), allowing for higher and higher resolution photos to be taken for the same price camera.[14]

- **Night vision.** Infrared and ultraviolet imaging enable night vision by capturing light outside the spectrum visible to the human eye. Infrared imaging (also known as thermal imaging) shows heat emitted by an object, and so is especially suited for identifying humans and animals in the dark.[15] Ultraviolet (UV) imaging can detect some materials not visible in natural or infrared light, and can also be used to enhance detail; for instance, it can be used to image surface textures not apparent in visible light.[16] Moving forward, thermal imaging is likely to improve—for example becoming more sensitive and available at higher resolutions.

- **See-through imaging.** The military is developing radar technologies that can see through ceilings and walls and allow the tracking of human targets even when they are inside buildings.[17] A technology called Synthetic Aperture Radar, for example, can see through cloudy and dusty conditions and through foliage, and has the potential to penetrate the earth and walls.[18]

- **Video analytics.** This field seeks to apply artificial intelligence techniques not just to collect but also to "watch" video. The technology has been improving rapidly, and can

---

[14] Nathan Myhrvold, "Moore's Law Corollary: Pixel Power," New York Times, June 7, 2006, online at http://www.nytimes.com/2006/06/07/technology/circuits/07essay.html. Moore's law is the observation that the number of transistors that can be placed on an integrated circuit—and therefore broadly speaking the power of computers—doubles approximately every two years. It has held true for over 50 years.

[15] NASA Science Mission Directorate, "Infrared Energy," Mission: Science, 2010, online at http://missionscience.nasa.gov/ems/07_infraredwaves.html.

[16] Austin Richards, "Digital Reflected-Ultraviolet Imaging," Advanced Imaging, Apr. 2006, online at http://www.uvcorder.com/pdf/ADI0406%20Component%2018-20.pdf.

[17] See e.g., William Saletan, "Nowhere To Hide," Slate.com, Sept. 17, 2008, online at http://www.slate.com/articles/health_and_science/human_nature/2008/09/nowhere_to_hide.html Greg Miller and Julian E. Barnes, "Special drones pursue militias," Los Angeles Times, Sept. 12, 2008, online at http://articles.latimes.com/2008/sep/12/world/fg-pakistan12

[18] "Ground Moving Target Indicator (GMTI) Radar Discrimination of Combatants versus Animals in Severe Clutter," DARPA, undated document (topic number SB082-019), online at http://www.dodsbir.net/sitis/archives_display_topic.asp?Bookmark=32303. Sandia National Laboratories, "Synthetic Aperture Radar Applications," undated, online at http://www.sandia.gov/radar/sarapps.html; Alicia Tejada, "MIT Develops New Radar Technology: Military Could See Through Walls," ABC News, Oct. 20, 2011, online at http://abcnews.go.com/Technology/radar-technology-mit-walls/story?id=14773871.

recognize and respond to specific people, events, and objects.[19] One of the most significant uses would be to continually track individuals or vehicles as they move about, using face recognition or other bodily characteristics.[20] It might also be used to identify particular movement patterns as "suspicious," or to identify and flag changes in routines, buildings or grounds.[21] Computers performing these tasks have a distinct advantage over human observers, because as one observer summed it up, "machines do not blink or forget. They are tireless assistants."[22]

The PBS series NOVA, "Rise of the Drones," recently aired a segment detailing the capabilities of a powerful aerial surveillance system known as ARGUS-IS. This system, which is basically a super-high, 1.8 gigapixel resolution camera that can be mounted on a drone, demonstrates many of these capacities. The system is capable of high-resolution monitoring and recording of an entire city. To see a demonstration of this capacity please see:
http://www.youtube.com/watch?feature=player_embedded&v=13BahrdkMU8

IV. UAVs and Possible Harms

With the federal government likely to permit more widespread use of drones, and the technology likely to become ever more powerful, the question becomes: what role will drones play in American life? Based on current trends—technology development, law enforcement interest, political and industry pressure, and the lack of legal safeguards—it is clear that drones pose a looming threat to Americans' privacy. The reasons for concern reach across a number of different dimensions:

- **Mission creep.** Even where UAVs are being envisioned for search and rescue, fighting wildfires, and in dangerous tactical police operations, they are likely to be quickly embraced by law enforcement around the nation for other, more controversial purposes. The police in Ogden, Utah think that floating a surveillance blimp above their city "will be a deterrent to crime when it is out and about."[23] In Houston, police suggested that drones could possibly be used for writing traffic tickets.[24] The potential result is that they become commonplace in American life.
- **Tracking.** The Justice Department currently claims the authority to monitor Americans' comings and goings using GPS tracking devices—without a warrant. Fleets of UAVs, interconnected and augmented with analytics software, could enable the mass tracking of vehicles and pedestrians around a wide area.

---

[19] Vigilant Video, online at http://www.vigilantvideo.com
[20] Noah Shachtman, "Army Tracking Plan: Drones That Never Forget a Face," *Wired.com*, Sept. 28, 2011, online at http://www.wired.com/dangerroom/2011/09/drones-never-forget-a-face/.
[21] On change detection, see Sandia National Laboratories, "Synthetic Aperture Radar Applications," undated, online at http://www.sandia.gov/radar/sarapps.html.
[22] Steve Lohr, "Computers That See You and Keep Watch Over You," *New York Times*, Jan. 1, 2011, online at http://www.nytimes.com/2011/01/02/science/02see.html.
[23] James Nelson, "Utah city may use blimp as anti-crime spy in the sky," Reuters, Jan. 16, 2011, online at http://www.reuters.com/article/2011/01/16/us-crime-blimp-utah-idUSTRE70F1DJ20110116.
[24] Stephen Dean, "Police line up to use drones on patrol after Houston secret test," Houston Examiner, Jan. 11, 2010, online at http://www.examiner.com/page-one-in-houston/police-line-up-to-use-drones-on-patrol-after-houston-secret-test.

- **New uses.** The use of drones could also be expanded from surveillance to actual intervention in law enforcement situations on the ground. Airborne technologies could be developed that could, for example, be used to control or dispel protesters (perhaps by deploying tear gas or other technologies), stop a fleeing vehicle, or even deploy weapons.[25]

In addition, drones raise many of the same issues that pervasive video surveillance brings in any context. For example:

- **Chilling effects.** What would be the effect on our public spaces, and our society as a whole, if everyone felt the keen eye of the government on their backs whenever they ventured outdoors? Psychologists have repeatedly found that people who are being observed tend to behave differently, and make different decisions, than when they are not being watched. This effect is so great that a recent study found that "merely hanging up posters of staring human eyes is enough to significantly change people's behavior."[26]

- **Voyeurism.** Video surveillance is susceptible to individual abuse, including voyeurism. In 2004, a couple making love on a dark nighttime rooftop balcony, where they had every reason to expect they enjoyed privacy, were filmed for nearly four minutes by a New York police helicopter using night vision. This is the kind of abuse that could become commonplace if drone technology enters widespread use. (Rather than apologize, NYPD officials flatly denied that this filming constituted an abuse, telling a television reporter, "this is what police in helicopters are supposed to do, check out people to make sure no one is ... doing anything illegal").[27]

- **Discriminatory targeting.** The individuals operating surveillance systems bring to the job all their existing prejudices and biases. In Great Britain, camera operators have been found to focus disproportionately on people of color. According to a sociological study of how the systems were operated, "Black people were between one-and-a-half and two-and-a-half times more likely to be surveilled than one would expect from their presence in the population."[28]

- **Institutional abuse.** In addition to abuse by the inevitable "bad apples" within law enforcement, there is also the danger of institutional abuse. Sometimes, bad policies are

---

[25] Joseph Nevins, "Robocop: Drones at Home," Boston Review, January/February 2011, online at http://www.bostonreview.net/BR36.1/nevins.php.
[26] Sander van der Linden, "How the Illusion of Being Observed Can Make You a Better Person," Scientific American, May 3, 2011, online at http://www.scientificamerican.com/article.cfm?id=how-the-illusion-of-being-observed-can-make-you-better-person; M. Ryan Calo, "People Can Be So Fake: A New Dimension to Privacy and Technology Scholarship," 114 Penn St. L. Rev. 809, online at http://www.pennstatelawreview.org/articles/114/114%20Penn%20St,%20L,%20Rev,%20809.pdf.
[27] "Did NYPD Cameras Invade A Couple's Privacy?" WCBS-TV report, Feb. 24, 2005, video no longer available online; Jim Dwyer, "Police Video Caught a Couple's Intimate Moment on a Manhattan Rooftop," New York Times, Dec. 22, 2005, online at http://www.nytimes.com/2005/12/22/nyregion/22rooftop.html.
[28] Clive Norris and Gary Armstrong, "The Unforgiving Eye: CCTV Surveillance in Public Spaces," Centre for Criminology and Criminal Justice at Hull University, 1997.

set at the top, and an entire law enforcement agency is turned toward abusive ends. That is especially prone to happen in periods of social turmoil and intense political conflict. During the labor, civil rights, and anti-Vietnam war movements of the 20th century, the FBI and other security agencies engaged in systematic illegal behavior against those challenging the status quo. And once again today we are seeing an upsurge in spying against peaceful political protesters across America.[29]

- **Automated enforcement.** Drones are part of a trend toward automated law enforcement, in which cameras and other technologies are used to mete out justice with little or no human intervention. This trend raises a variety of concerns, such as the fact that computers lack the judgment to fairly evaluate the circumstances surrounding a supposed violation, and may be susceptible to bugs and other software errors, or simply are not programmed to fairly and properly encapsulate the state of the law as passed by legislatures.[30]

One point that is often made about new surveillance technologies is that, while they may increase government surveillance of individuals, they can also increase individuals' ability to record the activities of officials, which can serve as a check on their power. Too often, however, the authorities seek to increase their surveillance over individuals (for example, by installing surveillance cameras throughout public spaces) while restricting individuals' ability to use that same technology as a check against their power (for example, by attempting to prevent individuals from videotaping police[31]). Already, security experts have started expressing concern that unmanned aircraft could be used for terrorism[32]—which naturally raises the question: will individuals be able to make use of the new technology for their own purposes, or will government seek a monopoly over the new technology by citing fears of its use for terrorism?

V. *The Fourth Amendment and the Use of Drones*

The Supreme Court has never taken a position on whether the Fourth Amendment places limits on government use of UAV surveillance. However, it allowed some warrantless aerial surveillance from *manned* aircraft.

- In the 1986 decision **California v. Ciraolo**, the Supreme Court focused on whether an individual has a privacy interest in being free from aerial surveillance of his backyard. The police had received a tip that Dante Ciraolo was growing marijuana in his backyard, but high fences prevented them from viewing his backyard from the street. The police borrowed a plane, flew it over the backyard and easily spotted marijuana plants growing there. Ciraolo argued that his Fourth Amendment rights were violated because the government did not get a warrant. The Court rejected this argument, explaining that there

---

[29] See ACLU "Spyfiles" web site at www.aclu.org/spyfiles.
[30] Danielle Keats Citron, "Technological Due Process," 85 Washington University Law Review 1249 (2008), online at http://lawreview.wustl.edu/inprint/85/6/Citron.pdf.
[31] See Jay Stanley, "You Have Every Right to Photograph That Cop," ACLU, online at http://www.aclu.org/free-speech/you-have-every-right-photograph-cop.
[32] Agence France Press, "Flying Robot Attacks 'Unstoppable' Say Experts," Agence France Press, May 11, 2006, available online at http://www.rense.com/general71/sspm.htm.

was no intrusion into his privacy because "[a]ny member of the public flying in this airspace who glanced down could have seen everything that these officers observed."[33]

- **Dow Chemical Co. v. United States**, also decided in 1986, the Supreme Court addressed whether the Environmental Protection Agency violated Dow's Fourth Amendment rights when it employed a commercial aerial photographer to use a precision aerial mapping camera to take photographs of a chemical plant. The Court found no violation, in part because the camera the EPA used was a "conventional, albeit precise, commercial camera commonly used in mapmaking," and "the photographs here are not so revealing of intimate details as to raise constitutional concerns." However, the Court suggested that the use of more sophisticated, intrusive surveillance might justify a different result. It wrote, "surveillance of private property by using highly sophisticated surveillance equipment not generally available to the public, such as satellite technology, might be constitutionally proscribed absent a warrant."[34]

- In **Florida v. Riley**, decided in 1989, the police had received a tip that Michael Riley was growing marijuana in a greenhouse on the property surrounding his home. The interior of the greenhouse was not visible from the ground outside the property, and the greenhouse had a ceiling, though two panels in the ceiling were missing. A police officer flew over the greenhouse and spotted marijuana through the openings in the roof. While no reasoning commanded a majority of the Court, four justices concluded that its decision in *Ciraolo* applied because Riley had left part of the greenhouse open to public view, and so the search was constitutional.[35]

Because of their potential for pervasive use in ordinary law enforcement operations and capacity for revealing far more than the naked eye, drones pose a more serious threat to privacy than do manned flights. There are good reasons to believe that they may implicate Fourth Amendment rights in ways that manned flights do not.

Government use of UAVs equipped with technology that dramatically improves on human vision or captures something humans cannot see (such thermal or x-ray images) should be scrutinized especially closely by the courts. This follows from the Supreme Court's statement in Dow Chemical that using sophisticated technology not generally available to the public may be considered a search under the Fourth Amendment. It is also suggested by the 2001 case *Kyllo v. United States*, in which the court rejected the use of thermal imaging devices to peer into a suspect's home without a warrant.[36]

Further, the Supreme Court has suggested that the pervasive or continuous use of a surveillance technology may heighten Fourth Amendment concerns. In *United States v. Knotts*, the Supreme Court addressed whether attaching primitive "beeper" tracking technology to a car violated the driver's Fourth Amendment rights.[37] Although it concluded that the use of the

---

[33] 476 U.S. 207 (1986).
[34] 476 U.S. 227 (1986).
[35] 488 U.S. 445 (1989).
[36] 533 U.S. 27 (2001).
[37] 460 U.S. 276, 283-84 (1983).

beeper in that case did not violate the Fourth Amendment, it held that if "such dragnet type law enforcement practices" as "twenty-four hour surveillance of any citizen of this country" ever arose, it would determine if different constitutional principles would be applicable.

Similarly, in *US v. Jones*, decided last year, a concurrence joined by 5 justices found that GPS tracking of a car implicated an individual's reasonable expectation of privacy and noted "society's expectation has been that law enforcement agents and others would not—and indeed, in the main, simply could not—secretly monitor and catalogue every single movement of an individual's car for a very long period."[38] While this decision may eventually play a role in regulating drone usage, the technology is moving far more rapidly than our jurisprudence, and it is critical that Congress not delay action, especially with a looming 2015 deadline set by the FAA Reauthorization Act.

VI. Recommendations

UAVs can be an extremely powerful surveillance tool, and their use must be subject to strict limitations, as should all government power. Like any tool, UAVs have the potential to be used for good or ill. With implementation of good privacy ground rules, our society can enjoy the benefits of this technology without having to worry about its darker potential. Placing reasonable limitations on law enforcement is by no means a new idea. For example authorities may take a thermal image of someone's home only when they get a warrant. Congress should impose appropriate rules, limits and regulations on UAVs as well in order to preserve the privacy Americans have always expected and enjoyed.

At a minimum, Congress should enact the following core measures to ensure that this happens:

- **Usage restrictions.** UAVs should be subject to strict regulation to ensure that their use does not eviscerate the privacy that Americans have traditionally enjoyed and rightly expect. Innocent Americans should not have to worry that their activities will be scrutinized by drones. To this end, the use of drones should be prohibited for indiscriminate mass surveillance, for example, or for spying based on First Amendment-protected activities. In general, drones should not be deployed except:

    o where there are specific and articulable grounds to believe that the drone will collect evidence relating to a specific instance of criminal wrongdoing or, if the drone will intrude upon non-public spaces where the government has obtained a warrant based on probable cause; or

    o where there is a geographically confined, time-limited emergency situation in which particular individuals' lives are at risk, such as a fire, hostage crisis, or person lost in the wilderness; or

---

[38] 132 S.Ct. 945.

- for reasonable non-law enforcement purposes by non-law enforcement agencies, where privacy will not be substantially affected, such as geological inspections or environmental surveys, and where the surveillance will not be used for secondary law enforcement purposes.

- **Image retention restrictions.** Images of identifiable individuals captured by aerial surveillance technologies should not be retained or shared unless there is reasonable suspicion that the images contain evidence of criminal activity or are relevant to an ongoing investigation or pending criminal trial.

- **Public notice.** The policies and procedures for the use of aerial surveillance technologies should be explicit and written, and should be subject to public review and comment. While it is legitimate for the police to keep the details of particular investigations confidential, policy decisions regarding overall deployment policies—including the privacy trade-offs they may entail—are a public matter that should be openly discussed.

- **Democratic control.** Deployment and policy decisions surrounding UAVs should be democratically decided based on open information—not made on the fly by police departments simply by virtue of federal grants or other autonomous purchasing decisions or departmental policy fiats.

- **Auditing and effectiveness tracking.** Investments in UAVs should only be made with a clear, systematic examination of the costs and benefits involved. And if aerial surveillance technology is deployed, independent audits should be put in place to track the use of UAVs by government, so that citizens and other watchdogs can tell generally how and how often they are being used, whether the original rationale for their deployment is met, whether they represent a worthwhile public expenditure, and whether they are being used for improper or expanded purposes.

- **Ban on weaponization.** Weapons developed on the battlefield in Iraq and Afghanistan have no place inside the U.S. The national consensus on this issue is reflected by the fact that the Heritage Foundation and the International Association of Chiefs of Police join us in supporting sharp limits on weaponized drones.[39]

While this new technology certainly has beneficial uses – for search and rescue missions, firefighting, dangerous police tactical operations – it also poses significant possible harms if left unchecked. Drones should only be used if subject to a powerful framework that regulates their use in order to avoid abuse and invasions of privacy. The ACLU is eager to work with the members of this committee in order to create a robust and appropriate framework for drone use.

---

[39] International Assocation of Cheifs of Police, Aviation Committee, Recommended Guidelines for the use of Unmanned Aircraft. August 2012, see: http://www.theiacp.org/portals/0/pdfs/IACP_UAGuidelines.pdf; Paul Rosenzweig, Steven P. Bucci, Ph.D., Charles "Cully" Stimson and James Jay Carafano, Ph.D., *Drones in U.S. Airspace: Principles for Governance*, The Heritage Foundation, September 20, 2012, see: http://www.heritage.org/research/reports/2012/09/drones-in-us-airspace-principles-for-governance

Statement of Senator John Cornyn

Senate Judiciary Committee Hearing Entitled: *"Drones in America: Law Enforcement and Privacy Considerations"*

Technological innovation has driven incredible economic growth in the United States, and has improved nearly every aspect of our lives. But new technologies, especially when used inappropriately, can raise serious privacy concerns. The use of unmanned aerial surveillance systems in the United States brings these issues to the forefront, and I am glad we are holding this hearing to learn more about them.

In Texas, the United States Border Patrol has used unmanned aerial surveillance systems to help apprehend thousands of illegal immigrants and criminals on the Southern Border. Congress must ensure that these unmanned aerial surveillance systems are only used for legitimate national security and law enforcement purposes, and never used to harass, intimidate, or infringe upon the rights of United States citizens.

-30-

United States Senate Committee on the Judiciary

"The Future of Drones In America: Law Enforcement and Privacy Considerations"

March 20, 2013

WRITTEN STATEMENT OF RYAN CALO
ASSISTANT PROFESSOR
UNIVERSITY OF WASHINGTON SCHOOL OF LAW

Thank you Chairman Leahy, ranking Member Grassley, and Members of the Committee for this opportunity to testify today.

My name is Ryan Calo and I am a law professor at the University of Washington. I am also the former director for privacy and robotics at the Stanford Law School Center for Internet and Society.

Last year, Congress charged the Federal Aviation Administration (FAA) with accelerating the integration of unmanned aircraft systems—known colloquially as "drones"—into domestic airspace.[1] Drones are not new; we deployed them for target practice throughout World War II.[2] What is new is the prospect of their widespread use over American cities and towns.

Drones have a lot of people worried about privacy—and for good reason. Drones drive down the cost of aerial surveillance to worrisome levels. Unlike fixed cameras, drones need not rely on public infrastructure or private partnerships. And they can be equipped not only with video cameras and microphones, but also the capability to sense heat patterns, chemical signatures, or the presence of a concealed firearm.

American privacy law, meanwhile, places few limits on aerial surveillance. We enjoy next to no reasonable expectation of privacy in public, or from a public vantage like the nation's airways. The Supreme Court has made it clear through a series of decisions in the nineteen-eighties that there is no search for Fourth Amendment purposes if an airplane or helicopter permits officers to peer into your backyard.[3] I see no reason why these precedents would not extend readily to drones.

---

[1] FAA Modernization and Reform Act of 2012, P.L. 112-95, 126 Stat. 11.

[2] LAWRENCE NEWCOME, UNMANNED AVIATION: A BRIEF HISTORY OF UNMANNED AERIAL VEHICLES 48 (2004).

[3] *See* Florida v. Riley, 488 U.S. 445 (1989); California v. Ciraolo, 476 U.S. 207 (1986); Dow Chem. Co. v. United States, 476 U.S. 227 (1986).

Drones may also follow people around from place to place, even after the recent decision of *United States v. Jones*.[4] *Jones* held that affixing a global positioning device to a vehicle for the purpose of tracking the location of the occupant is a search within the meaning of the Fourth Amendment. But it is far from certain how *Jones* would apply to surveillance by a drone, which need not be affixed to anything.

Citizens have no reasonable expectation of privacy in contraband. Dogs can sniff luggage or cars without triggering the Fourth Amendment because, courts assume, dogs only alert in the presence of narcotics or other illegal possessions.[5] A logical extension of this precedent, it seems to me, is that drones could fly around testing the air for drug particles and report back suspicious activity to law enforcement without ever implicating the Constitution.[6]

I have heard it suggested that the Supreme Court's decision in *Kyllo v. United States* involving thermal imaging limits how drones might be used for surveillance. *Kyllo* holds, in essence, that officers need probable cause to peer into the home using technology that is unavailable to the general public.[7] Setting aside whether drones would even draw a *Kyllo* analysis, the technology will indeed be available to the general public as soon as 2015 when the FAA relaxes its ban on commercial use.

The subject of today's hearing is drones and law enforcement. I pause only to note that, if anything, there are even fewer limits on the use of drones by individuals, corporations, or the press. The common law privacy torts such as intrusion upon seclusion tend to track the constitutional doctrine that there should be no expectation of privacy in public.[8] Some might go further and argue that the press (at least) has a free speech interest in using technology to cover newsworthy events.[9]

This combination of cheap, powerful surveillance and inadequate privacy law has understandably resulted in a backlash against drones, one further compounded by our association of the technology with the theatre of war.

---

[4] 132 S.Ct. 945 (2012).

[5] *See* Illinois v. Caballes, 543 U.S. 405 (2005); United States v. Place, 462 U.S. 696, 707 (1983) ("A 'canine sniff' by a well-trained narcotics detection dog, however, does not ... expose noncontraband items that otherwise would remain hidden from public view.").

[6] *See* Ryan Calo, *The Drone as Privacy Catalyst*, 64 STAN. L. REV. ONLINE 29, 31 (2011).

[7] Kyllo v. United States, 533 U.S. 27 (2001).

[8] *E.g.*, RESTATEMENT (SECOND) OF TORTS § 652B. *But see* Daily Democrat v. Graham, 276 Ala. 380, 381 (1964) (plaintiff—whose dress had been blown up by the wind in a public place—allowed to pursue privacy tort against defendant photographer).

[9] *Cf.* Glik v. Cunniffe, 655 F.3d 78 (1st Cir. 2011) (holding that a citizen has a First Amendment right to videotape police during course of his arrest). Thank you to Margot Kaminiski for this pointer.

This is in many ways a shame. Drones have the potential to be a transformative technology, helping governments, empowering civilians, and fostering innovation in countless ways. As the Congressional Research Service recently stated in a report, "the extent of [drone's] potential domestic application is bound only by human ingenuity."[10] Drones can be lifesavers in the hands of police and firefighters and flying smart phones in the hands of consumers and private industry.

I am very concerned that we will not realize the potential of this technology because we have been so remiss in addressing the legitimate privacy concerns that attend it. There are several ways the government could change this picture. Ideally, we would take the opportunity to finally drag privacy law into the twenty-first century by reexamining our outmoded doctrines. This is a slow process, but courts do seem to be making strides in recent years.

Several federal bills have proposed placing limits on drones. I think we should be very careful here for a few reasons. First, the problem is broader than unmanned aircraft systems: flight is not a prerequisite for threatening civil liberties. There are robots that climb the side of buildings, for instance, that would not be covered under the draft bills I've read. Second, there is likely some benefit to allowing individual states to adopt different approaches to drones and seeing what works and what does not.

There is one approach that I believe could act as stop-gap, and that is for Congress to instruct the FAA to take privacy into account as part of its mandate to integrate drones into domestic airspace.[11] The agency has been largely silent on the issue of privacy—only recently did members of the privacy community receive a letter from the FAA asking for input in connection with the selection of drone testing centers.

But the FAA could require public and eventually private applicants to furnish the agency with a plan to minimize their impact on privacy as part of the application. The agency could then consider the plan, and even withdraw the license for those who flout it. This might help allay reasonable concerns over drones in the short term while continuing to permit their innovative and lifesaving uses.

Thank you again for the opportunity to speak today. I look forward to your questions.

---

[10] Allison Dolan and Richard Thompson II, *Integration of Drones into Domestic Airspace: Selected Legal Issues*, CRS Report for Congress, R42940 (Jan. 30, 2013).

[11] Representative Ed Markey made this suggestion in the Drone Aircraft Privacy and Transparency Act of 2012 (H.R. 6766) and the Electronic Privacy Information Center has formally petitioned the FAA to adopt privacy safeguards.

Statement of Senator Patrick Leahy (D-Vt.),
Chairman, Senate Judiciary Committee,
Hearing On
"The Future of Drones in America: Law Enforcement and Privacy Considerations"
March 20, 2013

The focus of today's hearing is on the *domestic*, non-military use of drones. Recently, the debate about the use of unmanned aerial vehicles, or "drones", has largely focused on the lethal targeting of suspected terrorists, including Americans. I continue to have deep concerns about the constitutional and legal implications of such targeted killings. I have spoken with Senator Durbin, and next month he will chair a hearing in the Constitution subcommittee that will examine these issues carefully. In addition, I will continue to press the administration to provide this Committee with all relevant Office of Legal Counsel opinions related to the use of drones to conduct targeted killings.

As I noted at the beginning of this Congress, I am convinced that the domestic use of drones to conduct surveillance and collect other information will have a broad and significant impact on the everyday lives of millions of Americans going forward. Just in the last decade, technological advancements have revolutionized aviation to make this technology cheaper and more readily available. As a result, many law enforcement agencies, private companies, and individuals have expressed interest in operating drones in our national airspace. I should note that we are not talking just about the large Predator drones that are being used by the military or along our borders, but also about smaller, lightweight unmanned vehicles like this one – about which we will hear testimony later. With the Federal Aviation Administration (FAA) estimating as many as 30,000 drones like this operating in the national airspace by the end of this decade, Congress must carefully consider the policy implications of this fast-emerging technology.

During our discussion of the domestic use of drones, I know that we will hear about many of the unique advantages of using unmanned aircraft, as opposed to manned vehicles. Drones are able to carry out arduous and dangerous tasks that would otherwise be expensive or difficult for a human to undertake. For example, in addition to law enforcement surveillance, drones will potentially be used for scientific experiments, agricultural research, geological surveying, pipeline maintenance, and search and rescue missions.

While there may be many valuable uses for this new technology, the use of unmanned aircraft raises serious concerns about the impact on the constitutional and privacy rights of American citizens. The Department of Homeland Security, through Customs and Border Protection, already operates modified, unarmed drones to patrol rural parts of our northern and southern borders, as well as to support drug interdiction efforts by law enforcement. In addition, a growing number of local law enforcement agencies have begun to explore using drones to assist with operational surveillance. This raises a number of questions regarding the adequacy of current privacy laws and the scope of existing Fourth Amendment jurisprudence regarding aerial surveillance: When is it appropriate for law enforcement to use a drone, and for what purposes? Under what circumstances should law enforcement be required to first obtain a search warrant, and what should be done with the data that is collected? And although no drones operating in the

U.S. are yet weaponized, should law enforcement be permitted to equip unmanned aircraft with non-lethal tools such as tear gas or pepper spray?

My concerns about the domestic use of drones extend beyond government and law enforcement. Before we allow widespread commercial use of drones in the domestic airspace, we need to carefully consider the impact on the privacy rights of Americans. Just last week, we were reminded how one company's push to gather data on Americans can lead to vast over-collection and potential privacy violations. Similarly, a simple scan of amateur videos on the internet demonstrates how prevalent drone technology is becoming amongst private citizens. Small, quiet unmanned aircraft can easily be built or purchased online for only a few hundred dollars, and equipped with high-definition video cameras while flying in areas impossible for manned aircraft to operate without being detected. It is not hard to imagine the serious privacy problems that this type of technology could cause.

On this issue, we cannot take a short-sighted view, and we must realize that technology in this area will advance at an incredible rate. This topic is of significant interest to many members of our Committee, and I hope that this hearing will be just the beginning of an ongoing dialogue as to how best to manage the unique privacy threats associated with this modern technology, while not stifling this nascent industry that has enormous potential to improve our lives.

To help this Committee explore some of these issues, Senator Grassley and I have invited witnesses who will testify from a variety of perspectives. We will hear from a law enforcement official who has a functioning and fully operational unmanned aircraft unit, the head of the leading unmanned vehicle industry group, a representative from the Electronic Privacy Information Center, and a scholar who has studied the intersection of drone technology with privacy and Fourth Amendment law. I thank the witnesses for being with us today.

# # # # #

Written Testimony

Of

Benjamin Miller,
Unmanned Aircraft Program Manager,
Mesa County Sheriff's Office

and

Representative of the
Airborne Law Enforcement Association

Before the Committee on the Judiciary
United States Senate

For the Hearing:

"The Future of Drones in America: Law Enforcement and Privacy Considerations"

Good morning Chairman Leahy and members of the Committee. My name is Benjamin Miller, Unmanned Aircraft Program Manager with the Mesa County Sheriff's Office and Representative of the Airborne Law Enforcement Association.

Thank you for inviting me to speak to you about the use of unmanned aircraft in the small Colorado community where I live. The Mesa County Sheriff's Office is a middle sized agency employing approximately 200 people with a patrol team of just over 65 deputies. These deputies serve approximately 175,000 citizens who live inside a 3,300 square mile county. We see a wide range of criminal activity, from petty offenses to major crimes including drug trafficking and homicide.

Today, I speak to you not only on behalf of the Mesa County Sheriff's Office, but on behalf of the Airborne Law Enforcement Association (ALEA). The ALEA has guided our agency through the last four years of research and program genesis in the responsible use of unmanned aircraft. It is over these last four years that we've gained the experience using unmanned aircraft that I'd like to share with you today.

In four years, we have flown 185 hours in just over 40 missions with two small, battery operated unmanned aircraft systems. The Draganflyer X6 is a backpack sized helicopter that can fly for 15 minutes. Our small airplane, called Falcon UAV, can fly for an hour and can fit in the trunk of a car. Both systems are used to carry cameras.

I'd like to share with you today some examples of how we've used these systems to provide you with a picture of how unmanned aircraft are playing a role in our department's commitment to public safety.

My first example occurred last May when an historic church caught fire. We flew the Draganflyer X6, carrying a thermal camera which allowed us to show the hot spots that still needed to be properly extinguished. Firemen were then able to assess the situation and address it accordingly, as these areas were not viewable to the naked eye. We then flew a point and click camera, available at your neighborhood Walmart, about 60 feet in the air and took photos that the arson investigators were able to use to determine which direction the fire had traveled through the building.

My next example occurred a few weeks ago when a 62 year old woman was reported missing. We launched our Falcon UAV in an effort to find this woman. Flying all day, we were able to clear large areas in a short time that would normally take much longer and involve more resources. The woman's body was recovered by ground personnel the following day. The use of Falcon allowed us to more directly apply our resources in this recovery effort.

My final example occurred just days ago, has little to do with law enforcement, but it offers a glimpse as to the real benefit of unmanned aerial systems and that is, affordability. Each year, Mesa County spends nearly ten thousand dollars on a manned aerial survey of our landfill to determine the increase in waste over the previous year. My team and I completed that very same survey with our unmanned aircraft for a mere two hundred dollars in cost to the taxpayer. By flying back and forth over the landfill, using yet another low cost point and click camera, we were able to combine those photos with geographic reference data and provide a volume to the landfill to an accuracy of 10 cubic centimeters.

This example speaks to the real heart of what we've learned in the last few years. I must admit that when we started this project, I had thoughts of grandeur, chasing criminals across the landscape and solving all my community's public safety problems with state of the art technology seen on the news in Iraq and Afghanistan. Four years later, the reality is the equipment we use and the military "Drones" you see on TV have as much in common as a bicycle and a race car.

While military unmanned aircraft fly for hours and sometimes days at enormous altitudes, we fly just minutes to photograph a crime or accident scene and cannot exceed an hour of flight time, nor can we fly more than 400 feet above the ground we stand on. While military unmanned aircraft are both large in size and cost, our equipment is small and relatively inexpensive. Our equipment does not possess the capability to carry sensors that can read license plates from space or look into your home. Our small unmanned aerial vehicles cannot carry weapons nor do we have a desire to have them do so. Furthermore, we can only fly during daylight conditions and our vehicles must remain within line of sight of the operator.

On the other side of the spectrum from the large "predator-type drones," are the micro unmanned aerial vehicles which you may have seen in some internet and/or TV demonstrations, where numerous vehicles move in complex formations. While we can fearfully contemplate massive swarms of police drones covering the skies, such fears fail to consider simple variables such as wind, making such devices virtually irrelevant for unmanned airborne public safety missions.

Just recently, I was on the Airborne Law Enforcement Association's website and found a 1934 photo of an airborne police officer in a gyrocopter with a telegraph machine strapped to his leg. Aviation and public safety have a long standing relationship. While unmanned aircraft cannot recover a stranded motorist in a swollen river, they can provide an aerial view for a fraction of the cost of manned aviation. I estimate unmanned aircraft can complete 30 percent of the missions of manned aviation for 2 percent of the cost. The Mesa County Sheriff's Office projects direct cost of unmanned flight at just $25 an hour as compared to the cost of manned aviation that can range from $250 to thousands of dollars per hour. It actually costs just one cent to charge a flight battery for either of our systems.

The Airborne Law Enforcement Association embraces the conduct of public safety missions within the specified confines of our nation's laws at all levels of government -- federal, state, and local. We also embrace the introduction of new technologies, such as unmanned aerial systems, that support public safety missions. Additionally, we strongly support the Constitutional process of lawfully obtaining a search warrant when there are specific, articulable grounds to believe that the use of an aircraft, including unmanned aircraft, will intrude upon reasonable expectations of privacy. However, in situations where time is of the essence and no reasonable expectation of privacy exists, we would be opposed to restrictions that would limit the effectiveness of this technology. Further, the introduction of this new technology as a tool of public safety does not transfer to the notion that public safety officers, by virtue of the use of this new tool, will retract their oaths of office to uphold the laws of this nation, to include the laws that protect the privacy of its citizens.

In almost a century since law enforcement's first use of aviation, numerous judicial opinions have been handed down that uphold the Fourth Amendment's protections against unreasonable searches and seizures.

My agency's use of unmanned aircraft is primarily for search and rescue and crime scene reconstruction, but any tool can be abused. This sad reality is not unique to law enforcement, nor did it begin with unmanned aircraft. While the use of unmanned aircraft requires specific policies and procedures, the handling of sensitive photographs and video has been around law enforcement for many years. I can speak to a strong code of conduct policy inside my own agency that addresses more than just the use of unmanned aircraft. Leadership organizations like the International Association of Chiefs of Police have recently released unmanned aircraft policy guidelines that encourage agencies to adopt non-retention policies (see Exhibit 1), whereby agencies do not keep images that do not qualify as evidence. These guidelines have also been endorsed by the Airborne Law Enforcement Association (see Exhibit 2). It is with their guidance that agencies like mine are developing robust policies, quality training tools and professional unmanned aircraft programs.

In closing, I hope that my testimony has offered a realistic perspective of the many benefits unmanned aircraft can provide to public safety.

Thank you for the opportunity to speak with you today.

Exhibit 1

INTERNATIONAL ASSOCIATION OF CHIEFS OF POLICE

AVIATION COMMITTEE

Recommended Guidelines for the use of Unmanned Aircraft

BACKGROUND:

Rapid advances in technology have led to the development and increased use of unmanned aircraft. That technology is now making its way into the hands of law enforcement officers nationwide.

We also live in a culture that is extremely sensitive to the idea of preventing unnecessary government intrusion into any facet of their lives. Personal rights are cherished and legally protected by the Constitution. Despite their proven effectiveness, concerns about privacy threaten to overshadow the benefits this technology promises to bring to public safety. From enhanced officer safety by exposing unseen dangers, to finding those most vulnerable who may have wandered away from their caregivers, the potential benefits are irrefutable. However, privacy concerns are an issue that must be dealt with effectively if a law enforcement agency expects the public to support the use of UA by their police.

The Aviation Committee has been involved in the development of unmanned aircraft policy and regulations for several years. The Committee recommends the following guidelines for use by any law enforcement agency contemplating the use of unmanned aircraft.

DEFINITIONS:

1. **Model Aircraft** - A remote controlled aircraft used by hobbyists, which is manufactured and operated for the purposes of sport, recreation and/or competition.

2. **Unmanned Aircraft (UA)** – An aircraft that is intended to navigate in the air without an on-board pilot. Also called Remote Piloted Aircraft and "drones."

3. **UAS Flight Crewmember** - A pilot, visual observer, payload operator or other person assigned duties for a UAS for the purpose of flight.

4. **Unmanned Aircraft Pilot** - A person exercising control over an unmanned aircraft during flight.

COMMUNITY ENGAGEMENT:

1. Law enforcement agencies desiring to use UA should first determine how they will use this technology, including the costs and benefits to be gained.

2. The agency should then engage their community early in the planning process, including their governing body and civil liberties advocates.

3. The agency should assure the community that it values the protections provided citizens by the U.S. Constitution. Further, the agency will operate the aircraft in full compliance with the mandates of the Constitution, federal, state and local law governing search and seizure.

4. The community should be provided an opportunity to review and comment on agency procedures as they are being drafted. Where appropriate, recommendations should be considered for adoption in the policy.

5. As with the community, the news media should be brought into the process early in its development.

SYSTEM REQUIREMENTS:

1. The UAS should have the ability to capture flight time by individual flight and cumulative over a period of time. The ability to reset the flight time counter should be restricted to a supervisor or administrator.

2. The aircraft itself should be painted in a high visibility paint scheme. This will facilitate line of sight control by the aircraft pilot and allow persons on the ground to monitor the location of the aircraft. This recommendation recognizes that in some cases where officer safety is a concern, such as high risk warrant service, high visibility may not be optimal.

However, most situations of this type are conducted covertly and at night. Further, given the ability to observe a large area from an aerial vantage point, it may not be necessary to fly the aircraft directly over the target location.

3. Equipping the aircraft with weapons of any type is strongly discouraged. Given the current state of the technology, the ability to effectively deploy weapons from a small UA is doubtful. Further, public acceptance of airborne use of force is likewise doubtful and could result in unnecessary community resistance to the program.

4. The use of model aircraft, modified with cameras, or other sensors, is discouraged due to concerns over reliability and safety.

OPERATIONAL PROCEDURES:

1. UA operations require a Certificate of Authorization (CAO) from the Federal Aviation Administration (FAA). A law enforcement agency contemplating the use of UA should contact the FAA early in the planning process to determine the requirements for obtaining a COA.

2. UAS will only be operated by personnel, both pilots and crew members, who have been trained and certified in the operation of the system. All agency personnel with UA responsibilities, including command officers, will be provided training in the policies and procedures governing their use.

3. All flights will be approved by a supervisor and must be for a legitimate public safety mission, training, or demonstration purposes.

4. All flights will be documented on a form designed for that purpose and all flight time shall be accounted for on the form. The reason for the flight and name of the supervisor approving will also be documented.

5. An authorized supervisor/administrator will audit flight documentation at regular intervals. The results of the audit will be documented. Any changes to the flight time counter will be documented.

6. Unauthorized use of a UA will result in strict accountability.

7. Except for those instances where officer safety could be jeopardized, the agency should consider using a "Reverse 911" telephone system to alert those living and working in the vicinity of aircraft operations (if such a system is available). If such a system is not available, the use of patrol car public address systems should be considered. This will not only provide a level of safety should the aircraft make an uncontrolled landing, but citizens may also be able to assist with the incident.

8. Where there are specific and articulable grounds to believe that the UA will collect evidence of criminal wrongdoing and if the UA will intrude upon reasonable expectations of privacy, the agency will secure a search warrant prior to conducting the flight.

IMAGE RETENTION:

1. Unless required as evidence of a crime, as part of an on-going investigation, for training, or required by law, images captured by a UA should not be retained by the agency.

2. Unless exempt by law, retained images should be open for public inspection.

Exhibit 2

AIRBORNE LAW ENFORCEMENT ASSOCIATION

50 Carroll Creek Way, Suite 260 Frederick, MD 21701
Bus (301) 631-2406 Fax (301) 631-2466
www.alea.org

RESOLUTION

IN SUPPORT OF THE

INTERNATIONAL ASSOCIATION OF CHIEFS OF POLICE

AVIATION COMMITTEE'S

Recommended Guidelines for the use of Unmanned Aircraft

WHEREAS, the Airborne Law Enforcement Association (ALEA) is a non-profit public benefit corporation of the State of California whose primary purpose is to promote, develop, prepare, disseminate and evaluate information with respect to the safe utilization of aircraft as a tool of law enforcement and airborne law enforcement techniques, equipment, and philosophy as an educational service for members of the organization and the public; and,

WHEREAS, ALEA embraces new technologies, such as Unmanned Aerial Systems (UAS), that support public safety missions, and;

WHEREAS, ALEA embraces the conduct of public safety missions within the specified confines of our nation's laws, federal, state, and local; and

WHEREAS, ALEA recognizes that the introduction of UAS into the national airspace brings with it unique privacy concerns that threaten to overshadow the benefits of this technology;

THEREFORE BE IT RESOLVED THAT the Airborne Law Enforcement Association adopt and promote the International Association of Chiefs of Police Aviation Committee's *Recommended Guidelines for the use of Unmanned Aircraft*.

Adopted by the Airborne Law Enforcement Association Board of Directors on August 29, 2012.

Gregg Weitzman, ALEA Secretary

Kurt Frisz, ALEA President

epic.org
ELECTRONIC PRIVACY INFORMATION CENTER

Testimony and Statement for the Record of

Amie Stepanovich
Director of the Domestic Surveillance Project
Electronic Privacy Information Center

Hearing on "The Future of Drones in America:
Law Enforcement and Privacy Considerations"

Before the

Judiciary Committee
of the
U.S. Senate

March 20, 2013
226 Dirksen Senate Office Building
Washington, D.C.

Mister Chairman and Members of the Committee, thank you for the opportunity to testify today concerning the use of drones by law enforcement in the United States. My name is Amie Stepanovich. I am the Director of the Domestic Surveillance Project at the Electronic Privacy Information Center.

EPIC is a non-partisan research organization, established in 1994, to focus public attention on emerging privacy and civil liberties issues.[1] We work with a distinguished panel of advisors in the fields of law, technology, and public policy.[2] We have a particular interest in the protection of individual privacy rights against government surveillance. In the last several years, EPIC has taken a particular interest in the unique privacy problems associated with aerial drones.

The Federal Aviation Administration ("FAA") has been directed to fully integrate drones into the National Airspace by 2015.[3] In 2012 EPIC petitioned the FAA, as it considers new regulations to permit the widespread deployment of drones, to also develop new privacy safeguards.[4] The FAA heeded our warning, and is now considering privacy policies for drone operators. However, more must be done to protect the privacy of individuals in the United States.

We appreciate the Committee's interest in domestic drone use and its substantial impact on the privacy of individuals in the United States. In my statement today, I will describe the unique threats to privacy posed by drone surveillance, the problems with current legal safeguards, and the need for Congress to act.

I. Aerial Drones Pose a Unique Threat to Privacy

A drone is an aerial vehicle designed to fly without a human pilot on board. Drones can either be remotely controlled or autonomous. Drones can be weaponized and deployed for military purposes.[5] Drones can also be equipped with sophisticated surveillance technology that makes it possible to spy on individuals on the ground. In a report on drones published by EPIC in 2005, we observed, "the use of [drones] gives the federal government a new capability to monitor citizens clandestinely, while the effectiveness of the...surveillance planes in border patrol operations has not been proved."[6] Today, drones greatly increase the capacity for law enforcement to collect personal information on individuals.

---

[1] *About EPIC*, EPIC, http://www.epic.org/about (last visited July 16, 2012).
[2] *EPIC Advisory Board*, EPIC, http://www.epic.org/epic/advisory_board.html (last visited July 16, 2012).
[3] Federal Aviation Administration Modernization and Reform Act of 2012 ("FMRA"), Pub. L. 112-95 §§ 331-336 (2012), *available at* http://www.gpo.gov/fdsys/pkg/PLAW-112publ95/pdf/PLAW-112publ95.pdf.
[4] *Unmanned Aerial Vehicles (UAVs) and Drones*, EPIC, http://www.epic.org/privacy/drones (last visited July 16, 2012).
[5] *See, e.g., Predator B UAS*, General Atomics Aeronautical, http://www.ga-asi.com/products/aircraft/predator_b.php (last visited June 25, 2012); *X-47B UCAS*, Northrop Grumman, http://www.as.northropgrumman.com/products/nucasx47b/index.html (last visited July 16, 2012).
[6] *Spotlight on Surveillance: Unmanned Planes Offer New Opportunities for Clandestine Government Tracking* (August 2005), EPIC, http://epic.org/privacy/surveillance/spotlight/0805/ (last visited July 16, 2012).

We recognize that there are many positive applications for drones within the United States. With little to no risk to individual privacy, drones may be used to combat forest fires, conduct search and rescue operations, survey emergency situations, and monitor hurricanes and other weather phenomena.[7] In Dallas, a drone used by a hobbyist photographer was able to pinpoint an instance of gross environmental abuse at a nearby factory.[8] In Alabama, drones were recently used to assist in monitoring a hostage situation involving a young boy abducted off of the school bus.[9]

However, when drones are used to obtain evidence in a criminal proceeding, intrude upon a reasonable expectation of privacy, or gather personal data about identifiable individuals, rules are necessary to ensure that fundamental standards for fairness, privacy, and accountability are preserved.

The technology in use today is far more sophisticated than most people understand. Cameras used to outfit drones are among the highest definition cameras available. The Argus camera, featured on the PBS Nova documentary on drones, has a resolution of 1.8 gigapixels and is capable of observing objects as small as six inches in detail from a height of 17,000 feet.[10] On some drones, sensors can track up to 65 different targets across a distance of 65 square miles.[11] Drones may also carry infrared cameras, heat sensors, GPS, sensors that detect movement, and automated license plate readers.[12]

Recent records received by EPIC under the Freedom of Information Act demonstrate that the Bureau of Customs and Border Protection procured drones outfitted

---

[7] *See, e.g.*, Tim Wall, *Flying Drones Fight Fires*, Discovery News (Nov. 10, 2011), *available at* http://news.discovery.com/earth/flying-drones-fight-fires-111110.html; Meghan Keneally, *Drone Plane Spots a River of Blood Flowing From the Back of a Dallas Meat Packing Plant*, Daily Mail Online (Jan. 24, 2012), *available at* http://www.dailymail.co.uk/news/article-2091159/A-drone-plane-spots-river-blood-flowing-Dallas-meat-packing-plant.html; Sean Holstege, *Drones' Good Flies Hand in Hand with Bad, Experts Fear*, AZCentral (July 7, 2012), *available at* http://www.azcentral.com/12news/news/articles/2012/07/07/20120707arizona-unmanned-drones-concerns.html.

[8] Meghan Keneally, *Drone Plane Spots a River of Blood Flowing From the Back of a Dallas Meat Packing Plant*, Daily Mail Online (Jan. 24, 2012), *available at* http://www.dailymail.co.uk/news/article-2091159/A-drone-plane-spots-river-blood-flowing-Dallas-meat-packing-plant.html.

[9] *See Military Tactics, Equipment Helped Authorities End Alabama Hostage Standoff*, Fox News (Feb. 7, 2013), http://www.foxnews.com/us/2013/02/07/alabama-kidnapper-was-killed-in-firefight-during-storming-bunker-fbi-says/.

[10] Ryan Gallagher, *Could the Pentagon's 1.8 Gigapixel Drone Camera Be Used for Domestic Surveillance*, Slate (Feb. 6, 2013), http://www.slate.com/blogs/future_tense/2013/02/06/argus_is_could_the_pentagon_s_1_8_gigapixel_drone_camera_be_used_for_domestic.html.

[11] *Id.*

[12] Customs and Border Protection Today, Unmanned Aerial Vehicles Support Border Security (July/Aug. 2004), *available at* http://www.cbp.gov/xp/CustomsToday/2004/Aug/other/aerial_vehicles.xml.

with technology for electronic signals interception and human identification.[13] Following receipt of these documents, EPIC and a broad coalition of privacy and civil liberties organizations petitioned the CBP to suspend the domestic drone program, pending the establishment of privacy safeguards.[14]

Much of this surveillance technology could, in theory, be deployed on manned vehicles. However, drones present a unique threat to privacy. Drones are designed to maintain a constant, persistent eye on the public to a degree that former methods of surveillance were unable to achieve. Drones are cheaper to buy, maintain, and operate than helicopters, or other forms of aerial surveillance.[15] Drone manufacturers have recently announced new designs that would allow drones to operate for more than 48 consecutive hours,[16] and other technology could extend the flight time of future drones into spans of weeks and months.[17] Also, "by virtue of their design, size, and how high they can fly, [drones] can operate undetected in urban and rural environments."[18]

Drones are currently being developed that will carry facial recognition technology, able to remotely identify individuals in parks, schools, and at political gatherings.[19] The ability to link facial recognition capabilities on drones operated by the Department of Homeland Security ("DHS") to the Federal Bureau of Investigation's Next Generation Identification database or DHS' IDENT database, two of the largest collections of biometric data in the world, further exacerbates the privacy risks.[20]

---

[13] Declan McCullagh, *DHS Built Domestic Surveillance Tech into Predator Drones*, CNET (Mar. 2, 2013), http://news.cnet.com/8301-13578_3-57572207-38/dhs-built-domestic-surveillance-tech-into-predator-drones/.
[14] Letter from the Electronic Privacy Information Center, et al. to David V. Aguilar, Deputy Commissioner, U.S. Bureau of Customs and Border Protection (Mar. 19, 2013), *available at* http://epic.org/drones_petition/.
[15] Nick Wingfield and Somini Sengupta, *Drones Set Sights on U.S. Skies*, NY Times (Feb. 17, 2012), *available at* http://www.nytimes.com/2012/02/18/technology/drones-with-an-eye-on-the-public-cleared-to-fly.html?pagewanted=all; http://www.wired.com/autopia/2012/05/drone-auto-vids/; Sabrina Hall, *Shelby County Sheriff's Department Wants Drones*, WREG (May 3, 2012), *available at* http://wreg.com/2012/05/03/shelby-county-sheriffs-department-wants-drones/. Drones can run from $300 for the most basic drone, able to record and transmit video, to $18 million for a General Atomics Predator B drone, the model owned by the United States Bureau of Customs and Border Protection. *See Parrot AR.Drone 2.0*, Apple, http://store.apple.com/us/product/H8859ZM/A (last visited July 16, 2012); Office of the Inspector Gen., Dep't Homeland Security, OIG-12-85, *CBPs Use of Unmanned Aircraft Systems in the Nation's Border Security* (May 2012), *available at* http://www.oig.dhs.gov/assets/Mgmt/2012/OIG_12-85_May12.pdf [hereinafter *DHS OIG Report*] at 2.
[16] Mark Brown, *Lockheed Uses Ground-Based Laser to Recharge Drone Mid-Flight* (July 12, 2012), *available at* http://www.wired.co.uk/news/archive/2012-07/12/lockheed-lasers.
[17] Steven Aftergood, *Secret Drone Technology Barred by "Political Conditions"* (Mar. 22, 2012), *available at* http://www.fas.org/blog/secrecy/2012/03/sandia_drone.html.
[18] Jennifer Lynch, *Are Drones Watching You?*, Electronic Frontier Foundation (Jan. 10, 2012), *available at* https://www.eff.org/deeplinks/2012/01/drones-are-watching-you.
[19] Clay Dillow, *Army Developing Drones that Can Recognize Your Face From a Distance*, PopSci (Sept. 28, 2011, 4:01 PM), http://www.popsci.com/technology/article/2011-09/army-wants-drones-can-recognize-your-face-and-read-your-mind.
[20] *See Next Generation Identification*, Federal Bureau of Investigation, http://www.fbi.gov/about-us/cjis/fingerprints_biometrics/ngi/ngi2/ (last visited July 16, 2012); Privacy Impact Assessment,

Law enforcement offices across the country have expressed interest in the purchase and use of drone technology to assist with law enforcement operations. Records released in 2012 by the Federal Aviation Administration show that over 220 public entities have already received approval to operate drones over the United States, including Police departments from Texas, Kansas, Washington, and other states.[21] The Florida Police Chiefs Association expressed a desire to use drones to conduct general crowd surveillance at public events.[22] News reports demonstrate that other police departments are not only interested in invasive surveillance equipment, but have also voiced interest in outfitting drones with non-lethal weapons.[23]

II. Current Privacy Safeguards are Inadequate

The Supreme Court has not yet considered the limits of drone surveillance under the Fourth Amendment, though the Court held twenty years ago that law enforcement may conduct manned aerial surveillance operations from as low as 400 feet without a warrant.[24] In addition, no federal statute currently provides adequate safeguards to protect privacy against increased drone use in the United States. Accordingly, there are substantial legal and constitutional issues involved in the deployment of aerial drones by law enforcement and state and federal agencies that need to be addressed. Technologist and security expert Bruce Schneier observed earlier this year at an event hosted by EPIC on Drones and Domestic Surveillance, "today's expensive and rare is tomorrow's commonplace."[25] As drone technology becomes cheaper and more common, the threat to privacy will become more substantial. High-rise buildings, security fences, or even the walls of a building are not barriers to increasingly common drone technology.

The Supreme Court is aware of the growing risks to privacy resulting from new surveillance technology but has yet to address the specific problems associated with drone surveillance. In *United States v. Jones*, a case that addressed whether the police could use a GPS device to track the movement of a criminal suspect without a warrant, the Court found

---

Department of Homeland Security, Automated Biometric Identification System (IDENT) (July 31, 2006), http://www.dhs.gov/xlibrary/assets/privacy/privacy_pia_usvisit_ident_final.pdf.

[21] *See* letter from Michael Huerta, Acting Administrator, Federal Aviation Administration to the Honorable Edward J. Markey (Sept. 21, 2012), *available at* http://markey.house.gov/sites/markey.house.gov/files/documents/FAA%20drones%20response.pdf; *see also* Jennifer Lynch, *Just How Many Drone Licenses Has the FAA Really Issued*, Electronic Frontier Foundation (Feb. 21, 2013), https://www.eff.org/deeplinks/2013/02/just-how-many-drone-licenses-has-faa-really-issued (providing details on contradictory statements made by the Federal Aviation Adminstration regarding the issuance of drone licenses).

[22] *See Florida Ban on Drones Advances Despite Law Enforcement Objections*, Fox News (Feb. 7, 2013), http://www.foxnews.com/politics/2013/02/07/fla-police-want-to-use-drones-for-crowd-control/.

[23] *See* Conor Friedersdorf, *Congress Should Ban Armed Drones Before Cops in Texas Deploy One*, the Atlantic (May 24, 2012), http://www.theatlantic.com/national/archive/2012/05/congress-should-ban-armed-drones-before-cops-in-texas-deploy-one/257616/.

[24] *See Florida v. Riley*, 488 U.S. 445 (1989) (holding that a police helicopter flying more than 400 feet above private property is not a search).

[25] Drones and Domestic Surveillance, EPIC, http://epic.org/events/drones/ (last visited Mar. 15, 2013).

that the installation and deployment of the device was an unlawful search and seizure.[26] Justice Sotomayor in a concurrence pointed to broader problems associated with new forms of persistent surveillance.[27] And Justice Alito, in a separate concurrence joined by three other Justices, wrote, "in circumstances involving dramatic technological change, the best solution to privacy concerns may be legislative."[28]

Regarding the invasive use of drones by commercial operators, current law does not anticipate the use of mobile devices that can hover outside a bedroom window or follow a person down a street. Legal standards should be established to protect people from a violation of reasonable expectations of privacy, including surveillance in public spaces. In consideration legislation to address law enforcement use of drones, it would be appropriate also to establish privacy standards for the commercial use of drones.

III. Congress Should Establish Safeguards Related to the Use of Drones

As the Chairman has indicated, the privacy and security concerns arising from the use of drones needs to be addressed.[29] In order to mitigate the risk of increased use of drones in our domestic skies, Congress must pass targeted legislation, based on principles of transparency and accountability.

State and local governments have considered a wide array of laws and regulations to prevent abuses associated with drone technology.[30] A current survey demonstrates that over 30 states have proposed legislation to protect against unregulated drone surveillance of individuals.[31] Most of these bills mandate a warrant requirement for the collection of information by drones operated by law enforcement officials.[32] Other bills require

---

[26] *United States v. Jones*, 132 S.Ct. 945, 949 (2012). See also U.S. v. Jones, EPIC, http://epic.org/amicus/jones/.
[27] *Id.* at 954-57.
[28] *Id.* at 964.
[29] Press Release from Senator Patrick Leahy, *The Agenda of the Senate Judiciary Committee for the 113th Congress* (Jan. 16, 2013), *available at* http://www.leahy.senate.gov/press/113-sjc-agenda-speech (I am concerned about the growing use of drones by federal and local authorities to spy on Americans here at home. This fast-emerging technology is cheap and could pose a significant threat to the privacy and civil liberties of millions of Americans.").
[30] *See, e.g.*, Erika Neddenien, *ACLU Teams with Lawmaker to Push Regulation of Unmanned Drones in VA*, WTVR (July 12, 2012 http://wtvr.com/2012/07/12/aclu-working-with-lawmaker-to-push-regulation-of-unmanned-drones-in-va/ (last visited July 16, 2012); Press Release, Seattle City Council, Seattle City Council Committee to Discuss Drones in Seattle and the Issues they Present (May 1, 2012), *available at* http://council.seattle.gov/2012/05/01/seattle-city-council-committee-to-discuss-drones-in-seattle-and-the-issues-they-present/.
[31] Allie Bohm, *Status of Domestic Drone Legislation in the States*, American Civil Liberties Union (Mar. 14, 2013), http://www.aclu.org/blog/technology-and-liberty/status-domestic-drone-legislation-states.
[32] Allie Bohm, *Drone Legislation: What's Being Proposed in the States?*, American Civil Liberties Union (Mar. 6, 2013), http://www.aclu.org/blog/technology-and-liberty-national-security/drone-legislation-whats-being-proposed-states (Noting that states that have introduced a bill to require a warrant for police drone surveillance include Arizona, California, Florida, Georgia, Idaho, Illinois, Kentucky, Maryland, Massachusetts, Minnesota, Missouri, Montana, New Hampshire, New Mexico, North Dakota, Oklahoma, Oregon, Rhode Island, South Carolina, Tennessee, Texas, Washington, and Wyoming.).

reporting requirements for drone operators.[33] A bill in Georgia restricts law enforcement use of drones strictly to felony investigations,[34] and a bill circulating in Oregon would require state approval for all drones, including federal drones, that would fly over the state's airspace.[35]

Even as states consider these various measures, it would be appropriate for Congress to establish privacy standards for the operation of drones in the United States. First, Congress should require all drone operators, both public and commercial, to submit, prior to receipt of a drone license, a detailed report on the drones' intended use. This report should describe, the specific geographic are where the drone will be deployed, the mission that the drone is expected to fulfill, and the surveillance equipment with which the drone will be outfitted. Each of these reports should be made publicly available at a publicly accessible web site. A private right of action and, in certain instances, federal prosecution authority should be included to ensure that drone operators comply with the terms of these statements.

In order to prevent abuses associated with the use of this technology, a strict warrant requirement needs to be implemented for all drone surveillance conduct by law enforcement. A warrant requirement would establish a presumption that evidence obtained by means of an aerial search should require judicial approval. Statutory exceptions could be created for exigency in order to address drone use in emergency situations or when necessary to protect human life. In addition, mandatory public reporting requirements, similar to those required by the Wiretap Act, would increase the transparency and accountability of law enforcement drone operations.[36]

Ongoing surveillance of individuals by aerial drones operating in domestic airspace should be prohibited. The invasiveness of drone technology represents a privacy risks to individuals as they pursue their daily activities. A drone, with the capability of staying aloft for hours or days at a time, could monitor a person's entire life as they go from home to work to school to the store and back. Even if law enforcement is not able to immediately discern exactly what a person says or does or buys at a particular location, simply tracking an individual's public movements in a systematic fashion for extended periods of time can create a vivid description of their private life.[37] Broad, unregulated drone surveillance would have a chilling effect on the speech and expression rights of individuals in the United States. Drones should not be used as robotic patrol officers for law enforcement.

Finally, drone surveillance technology may allow the collection of information and images that would otherwise be inaccessible to prying eyes, such as activities within the home. Congress should prohibit drone operators from conducting surveillance of

---

[33] *See id.* (Noting that states that have introduced a bill that includes a reporting requirement include Hawaii, Illinois, Maine, Mass, Rhode Island, Washington.).
[34] *See id.*
[35] Oregon SB 71 (2013), *available at* www.leg.state.or.us/13reg/measures/sb0001.dor/sb0071.intro.html.
[36] *See* 18 U.S.C. § 2519.
[37] *See* EPIC: Locational Privacy, https://epic.org/privacy/location_privacy/default.html.

individuals that infringes on property rights. A federal "Peeping Tom" statute, recognizing the enhanced capabilities of aerial drones, would provide baseline privacy protection for individuals within the home. Additional provisions should prevent against any use of drones to collect information that would not otherwise be retrievable without a physical trespass.

Additional drone legislation should include:

- Use Limitations – Prohibitions on general surveillance that limit law enforcement drone surveillance to specific, enumerated circumstances, such as in the case of criminal surveillance subject to a warrant, a geographically-confined emergency, or for reasonable non-law enforcement use where privacy will not be substantially affected;

- Data Retention Limitations – Restrictions on retaining or sharing surveillance data collected by drones, with emphasis on personally identifiable information;

- Transparency and Public Accountability – A requirement for all federal agencies that choose to operate drones to promulgate privacy regulations, subject to the notice and comment provisions of the Administrative Procedure Act. In addition, the law should provide for third party audits and oversight for law enforcement drone operations.

These three principles would further help protect the privacy interests of individuals against both government and commercial drone operators.

IV. Conclusion

The increased use of drones to conduct surveillance in the United States must be accompanied by increased privacy protections. The current state of the law is insufficient to address the drone surveillance threat. EPIC supports legislation aimed at strengthening safeguards related to the use of drones as surveillance tools and allowing for redress for drone operators who fail to comply with the mandated standards of protection. We also support compliance with the Administrative Procedure Act for the deployment of drone technology and limitations for federal agencies and other organizations that initially obtain a drone for one purpose and then wish to expand that purpose.

Thank you for the opportunity to testify today. I will be pleased to answer your questions.

AUVSI
ASSOCIATION FOR UNMANNED
VEHICLE SYSTEMS INTERNATIONAL

OPENING STATEMENT OF MICHAEL TOSCANO
PRESIDENT & CEO
ASSOCIATION FOR UNMANNED VEHICLE SYSTEMS INTERNATIONAL (AUVSI)

Senate Judiciary Committee Hearing
"The Future of Drones in America: Law Enforcement and Privacy Considerations"
March 20, 2013

Chairman Leahy and Ranking Member Grassley, I want to thank you and the rest of the Members of the Judiciary Committee for inviting me to testify here today.

My organization, the Association for Unmanned Vehicle Systems International – or AUVSI – is the world's largest non-profit organization devoted exclusively to advancing the unmanned systems and robotics community. We have more than 7,500 members, including more than 6,300 members in the United States. The industry is at the forefront of a technology that will not only benefit society, but the U.S. economy, as well. Earlier this month, my organization released a study, which found the unmanned aircraft industry is poised to help create 70,000 new jobs and $13.6 billion in economic impact in the first three years following the integration of unmanned aircraft into the national airspace.

However, the industry fully understands the technology is new to many Americans, and their opinions are being formed by what they see in the news. Today's hearing is an excellent opportunity to address some misconceptions about the technology and discuss how it will actually be used domestically.

You have probably noticed that I do not use the term "drone." The industry refers to the technology as unmanned aircraft systems, or UAS, because they are more than just a pilotless vehicle. A UAS also includes the technology on the ground, with a human at the controls. As I like to say, there is nothing unmanned about an unmanned system.

The term "drone" also carries with it a hostile connotation and does not reflect how UAS are actually being used domestically. UAS are used to perform dangerous and difficult tasks safely and efficiently. They were used to assess the flooding of the Red River in the upper Midwest. They were used to help battle California wildfires. And they are being used to study everything from hurricanes in the Gulf of Mexico, tornadoes in the Great Plains, and volcanoes in Hawaii.

Unlike military UAS, the systems most likely be used by public safety agencies are small systems, many weighing less than 5 pounds, with limited flight duration. As for weaponization, it is a non-starter. The FAA prohibits deploying weapons on civil aircraft. And for the record: AUVSI does not support the weaponization of civil UAS.

I also want to correct the misperception there is no regulation of domestic UAS. The FAA strictly regulates who, where, when, and why unmanned aircraft may be flown. If public entities want to fly UAS, they must obtain a Certificate of Authorization or COA from the FAA. UAS are generally flown within line of sight of the operator, lower than 400 feet, and during daylight hours. It is also currently a violation of FAA regulations to fly a UAS for commercial purposes.

As we focus on the use of UAS by law enforcement, it is important to recognize the robust legal framework already in place, rooted in the Fourth Amendment to our Constitution and decades of case law, which regulates how law enforcement uses any technology – whether it is unmanned aircraft, manned aircraft, thermal imaging, GPS, or cell phones.

Safeguarding people's privacy is important to my industry, as well. Last year, AUVSI published a Code of Conduct explicitly directing users to respect individual privacy. AUVSI also endorsed guidelines published by the International Association of Chiefs of Police for the use of unmanned aircraft by law enforcement. These guidelines were not only praised by our industry, but the ACLU as well. AUVSI strongly opposes any misuse of UAS technology. Just like with any technology, those who abuse it should be held accountable.

In conclusion, AUVSI believes all stakeholders can work together to advance this technology in a thoughtful way that recognizes the benefits and fuels job creation, while protecting Americans' safety, as well as their rights. Thank you, and I look forward to your questions.

United States Senate Committee on the Judiciary

"The Future of Drones In America: Law Enforcement and Privacy Considerations"

March 20, 2013

WRITTEN STATEMENT OF RYAN CALO
ASSISTANT PROFESSOR
UNIVERSITY OF WASHINGTON SCHOOL OF LAW

Thank you Chairman Leahy, ranking Member Grassley, and Members of the Committee for this opportunity to testify today.

My name is Ryan Calo and I am a law professor at the University of Washington. I am also the former director for privacy and robotics at the Stanford Law School Center for Internet and Society.

Last year, Congress charged the Federal Aviation Administration (FAA) with accelerating the integration of unmanned aircraft systems—known colloquially as "drones"—into domestic airspace.[1] Drones are not new; we deployed them for target practice throughout World War II.[2] What is new is the prospect of their widespread use over American cities and towns.

Drones have a lot of people worried about privacy—and for good reason. Drones drive down the cost of aerial surveillance to worrisome levels. Unlike fixed cameras, drones need not rely on public infrastructure or private partnerships. And they can be equipped not only with video cameras and microphones, but also the capability to sense heat patterns, chemical signatures, or the presence of a concealed firearm.

American privacy law, meanwhile, places few limits on aerial surveillance. We enjoy next to no reasonable expectation of privacy in public, or from a public vantage like the nation's airways. The Supreme Court has made it clear through a series of decisions in the nineteen-eighties that there is no search for Fourth Amendment purposes if an airplane or helicopter permits officers to peer into your backyard.[3] I see no reason why these precedents would not extend readily to drones.

---

[1] FAA Modernization and Reform Act of 2012, P.L. 112-95, 126 Stat. 11.

[2] LAWRENCE NEWCOME, UNMANNED AVIATION: A BRIEF HISTORY OF UNMANNED AERIAL VEHICLES 48 (2004).

[3] *See* Florida v. Riley, 488 U.S. 445 (1989); California v. Ciraolo, 476 U.S. 207 (1986); Dow Chem. Co. v. United States, 476 U.S. 227 (1986).

Drones may also follow people around from place to place, even after the recent decision of *United States v. Jones*.[4] *Jones* held that affixing a global positioning device to a vehicle for the purpose of tracking the location of the occupant is a search within the meaning of the Fourth Amendment. But it is far from certain how *Jones* would apply to surveillance by a drone, which need not be affixed to anything.

Citizens have no reasonable expectation of privacy in contraband. Dogs can sniff luggage or cars without triggering the Fourth Amendment because, courts assume, dogs only alert in the presence of narcotics or other illegal possessions.[5] A logical extension of this precedent, it seems to me, is that drones could fly around looking for unusual heat patterns or testing the air for drug particles and report back suspicious activity to law enforcement without ever implicating the Constitution.[6]

I have heard it suggested that the Supreme Court's decision in *Kyllo v. United States* involving thermal imaging limits how drones might be used for surveillance. *Kyllo* holds, in essence, that officers need probable cause to peer into the home using technology that is unavailable to the general public.[7] Setting aside whether drones would even draw a *Kyllo* analysis, the technology will indeed be available to the general public as soon as 2015 when the FAA relaxes its ban on commercial use.

The subject of today's hearing is drones and law enforcement. I pause only to note that, if anything, there are even fewer limits on the use of drones by individuals, corporations, or the press. The common law privacy torts such as intrusion upon seclusion tend to track the constitutional doctrine that there should be no expectation of privacy in public.[8] Some might go further and argue that the press (at least) has a free speech interest in using technology to cover newsworthy events.[9]

This combination of cheap, powerful surveillance and inadequate privacy law has understandably resulted in a backlash against drones, one further compounded by our association of the technology with the theatre of war.

---

[4] 132 S.Ct. 945 (2012).

[5] *See* Illinois v. Cabelles, 543 U.S. 405 (2005); United States v. Place, 462 U.S. 696, 707 (1983) ("A 'canine sniff' by a well-trained narcotics detection dog, however, does not ... expose noncontraband items that otherwise would remain hidden from public view.").

[6] *See* Ryan Calo, *The Drone as Privacy Catalyst*, 64 STAN. L. REV. ONLINE 29, 31 (2011).

[7] Kyllo v. United States, 533 U.S. 27 (2001).

[8] *E.g.*, RESTATEMENT (SECOND) OF TORTS § 652B. *But see* Daily Democrat v. Graham, 276 Ala. 380, 381 (1964) (plaintiff—whose dress had been blown up by the wind in a public place—allowed to pursue privacy tort against defendant photographer).

[9] *Cf.* Glik v. Cunniffe, 655 F.3d 78 (1st Cir. 2011) (holding that a citizen has a First Amendment right to videotape police during course of his arrest). Thank you to Margot Kaminisky for this pointer.

This is in many ways a shame. Drones have the potential to be a transformative technology, helping governments, empowering civilians, and fostering innovation in countless ways. As the Congressional Research Service recently stated in a report, "the extent of [drone's] potential domestic application is bound only by human ingenuity."[10] Drones can be lifesavers in the hands of police and firefighters and flying smart phones in the hands of consumers and private industry.

I am very concerned that we will not realize the potential of this technology because we have been so remiss in addressing the legitimate privacy concerns that attend it. There are several ways the government could change this picture. Ideally, we would take the opportunity to finally drag privacy law into the twenty-first century by reexamining our outmoded doctrines. This is a slow process, but courts do seem to be making strides in recent years.

Several federal bills have proposed placing limits on drones. I think we should be very careful here for a few reasons. First, the problem is broader than unmanned aircraft systems: flight is not a prerequisite for threatening civil liberties. There are robots that climb the side of buildings, for instance, that would not be covered under the draft bills I've read. Second, there is likely some benefit to allowing individual states to adopt different approaches to drones and seeing what works and what does not.

There is one approach that I believe could act as stop-gap, and that is for Congress to instruct the FAA to take privacy into account as part of its mandate to integrate drones into domestic airspace.[11] The agency has been largely silent on the issue of privacy—only recently did members of the privacy community receive a letter from the FAA asking for input in connection with the selection of drone testing centers.

But the FAA could require public and eventually private applicants to furnish the agency with a plan to minimize their impact on privacy as part of the application. The agency could then consider the plan, and even withdraw the license for those who flout it. This might help allay reasonable concerns over drones in the short term while continuing to permit their innovative and lifesaving uses.

Thank you again for the opportunity to speak today. I look forward to your questions.

---

[10] Allison Dolan and Richard Thompson II, *Integration of Drones into Domestic Airspace: Selected Legal Issues*, CRS Report for Congress, R42940 (Jan. 30, 2013).

[11] Representative Ed Markey made this suggestion in the Drone Aircraft Privacy and Transparency Act of 2012 (H.R. 6766) and the Electronic Privacy Information Center has formally petitioned the FAA to adopt privacy safeguards.

AUVSI
ASSOCIATION FOR UNMANNED
VEHICLE SYSTEMS INTERNATIONAL

Unmanned Aircraft Systems Privacy Statement

Unmanned Aircraft Systems (UAS) increase human potential by doing dangerous or difficult tasks safely and efficiently. Whether it is improving agriculture practices and output, helping first responders, advancing scientific research, or making business more efficient, UAS are capable of **saving time, saving money and most importantly, saving lives.**

The Association for Unmanned Vehicle Systems International (AUVSI) supports the development and advancement of UAS technology in a safe and responsible manner, while respecting existing privacy laws and ensuring transparency and accountability. AUVSI does not support additional restrictive legislation that will prohibit, delay, or prevent the use of UAS by our public safety agencies and other end users. AUVSI recognizes this new industry is poised to create over 70,000 new jobs within the first three years of UAS being integrated into the National Airspace System in the United States; however, restrictive legislation will inhibit this new industry.

AUVSI supports:

- Registration of unmanned aircraft and pilots with the Federal Aviation Administration (FAA).
- Enforcement of established law and policy, governing the collection, use, storage, sharing and deletion of data, regardless of how it is collected.
    - These policies should be available for public review.
    - The policies should outline strict accountability for unauthorized use.
    - AUVSI supports the International Association of Chiefs of Police recommended guidelines for UAS operations and their recommendations on data collection, which have been adopted by the Airborne Law Enforcement Association and others.
    - UAS manufacturers shall not be held responsible for improper or illegal use of unmanned aircraft systems.

AUVSI does not condone the use of UAS to illegally spy on people. AUVSI fully supports the prosecution of individuals that violate privacy laws. AUVSI fully supports the 4th Amendment's requirement that a search warrant be obtained prior to the government invading an individual's privacy.

AUVSI is opposed to many of the bills that have been introduced in Congress and at state capitals around the country. These bills would fundamentally change current search warrant requirements, which the courts have ably shaped over the past 225 years. The issue should be focused on the extent to which the government can collect, use and store personal data – which is why transparency and accountability are key.

Instead of focusing on how the government collects information, AUVSI supports an open debate on the government's right to collect, use, store, share, and delete personal data. AUVSI believes information gathered by a UAS should be treated no differently than information gathered by a manned aircraft, or other electronic means.

In 2012, AUVSI recently released the industry's first Code of Conduct which is built around safety, professionalism and respect.

AUVSI
ASSOCIATION FOR UNMANNED VEHICLE SYSTEMS INTERNATIONAL

Unmanned Aircraft System Operations

Industry "Code of Conduct"

The emergence of unmanned aircraft systems (UAS) as a resource for a wide variety of public and private applications quite possibly represents one of the most significant advancements to aviation, the scientific community, and public service since the beginning of flight. Rapid advancements in the technology have presented unique challenges and opportunities to the growing UAS industry and to those who support it. The nature of UAS and the environments which they operate, when not managed properly, can and will create issues that need to be addressed. The future of UAS will be linked to the responsible and safe use of these systems. Our industry has an obligation to conduct our operations in a safe manner that minimizes risk and instills confidence in our systems.

For this reason, the Association for Unmanned Vehicle Systems International (AUVSI), offers this Code of Conduct on behalf of the UAS industry for UAS operation. This code is intended to provide our members, and those who design, test, and operate UAS for public and civil use, a set of guidelines and recommendations for safe, non-intrusive operations. Acceptance and adherence to this code will contribute to safety and professionalism and will accelerate public confidence in these systems.

The code is built on three specific themes: Safety, Professionalism, and Respect. Each theme and its associated recommendations represent a "common sense" approach to UAS operations and address many of the concerns expressed by the public and regulators. This code is meant to provide UAS industry manufacturers and users a convenient checklist for operations and a means to demonstrate their obligation to supporting the growth of our industry in a safe and responsible manner. By adopting this Code, UAS industry manufacturers and users commit to the following:

Safety

- We will not operate UAS in a manner that presents undue risk to persons or property on the surface or in the air.
- We will ensure UAS will be piloted by individuals who are properly trained and competent to operate the vehicle or its systems.
- We will ensure UAS flights will be conducted only after a thorough assessment of risks associated with the activity. This risks assessment will include, but is not limited to:
  - Weather conditions relative to the performance capability of the system

99

- Identification of normally anticipated failure modes (lost link, power plant failures, loss of control, etc) and consequences of the failures
- Crew fitness for flight operations
- Overlying airspace, compliance with aviation regulations as appropriate to the operation, and off-nominal procedures
- Communication, command, control, and payload frequency spectrum requirements
- Reliability, performance, and airworthiness to established standards

Professionalism

- We will comply with all federal, state, and local laws, ordinances, covenants, and restrictions as they relate to UAS operations.
- We will operate our systems as responsible members of the aviation community.
- We will be responsive to the needs of the public.
- We will cooperate fully with federal, state, and local authorities in response to emergency deployments, mishap investigations, and media relations.
- We will establish contingency plans for all anticipated off-nominal events and share them openly with all appropriate authorities.

Respect

- We will respect the rights of other users of the airspace.
- We will respect the privacy of individuals.
- We will respect the concerns of the public as they relate to unmanned aircraft operations.
- We will support improving public awareness and education on the operation of UAS.

As an industry, it is incumbent upon us to hold ourselves and each other to a high professional and ethical standard. As with any revolutionary technology, there will be mishaps and abuses; however, in order to operate safely and gain public acceptance and trust, we should all act in accordance with these guiding themes and do so in an open and transparent manner. We hope the entire UAS industry will join AUVSI in adopting this industry Code of Conduct.

AUVSI
ASSOCIATION FOR UNMANNED
VEHICLE SYSTEMS INTERNATIONAL

2700 South Quincy Street, Suite 400 • Arlington, VA 22206 • 703.845.9671 • 703.845.9679 fax

Unmanned aircraft systems (UAS) help accomplish dangerous or difficult tasks safely and efficiently. Whether it is helping first responders, advancing scientific research, or making business more efficient, UAS are capable of saving time, saving money and most importantly, saving lives. But unlike the UAS we typically see in media reports, the types of UAS that will be used domestically will weigh less than 25 lbs, with many weighing less than 5 lbs. with an endurance of 30-90 minutes in the air.

Legislation passed last year requires the FAA to safely integrate UAS into the U.S. national airspace system (NAS) by 2015. Public safety agencies may only fly UAS if they have received a "Certificate of Authorization," or COA, from the FAA and COAs clearly outline when, how and where these small UAS may fly. They must be flown within line of sight of the operator, below 400 feet and only during the daytime. Below are a few examples of small UAS used by public safety agencies:

Photo: USGS

The Raven
Weight: 4.2 pounds
Length: 3.0 feet
Endurance: 60-90 minutes*
Range: 10 kilometers*

The Qube
Weight: 5.5 pounds
Length: 3 feet
Endurance: 40 minutes*
Range: 1 kilometer*

Photo: AeroVironment

Photo: Mesa County Sherriff Department

The Draganflyer
Weight: 2.2 pounds
Length: 34.25 inches
Endurance: 90 minutes*
Range: 500 meters*

*Endurance and range will vary based on weather conditions, the size and weight of the camera and more.

Unmanned Aircraft Systems:
Current and Future Uses

Past/Current Uses

- **Enhancing Public Safety**
    - Fighting wildfires in California – In 2008, NASA assisted the state of California in fighting wildfires with the use of Ikhana, a UAS equipped with advanced technology. The information about the fires collected by Ilkhana was transmitted to command centers within minutes, and then distributed into the field giving firefighters crucial situational awareness. Throughout the operation, NASA pilots operating Ilkhana were in close communication with the FAA to ensure its safe separation from other aircraft.

    - Finding missing persons in New Mexico – On January 9, 2012, an Oklahoma couple became lost in the White Sands National Monument in New Mexico. UAS were brought in to assist with the search. Once the couple's location was pinpointed, the UAS relayed specific coordinates of the couple and monitored their location and movement as rescue helicopters were en route.

    - Patrolling the U.S.-Mexico border – The U.S. Customs and Border Patrol use unmanned systems to patrol the U.S.-Mexico border, helping prevent drug smuggling and potential terrorist threats. The UAS monitor areas, which would take agents on the ground days to reach.

- **Enabling Scientific Research**
    - NASA studying hurricanes – NASA is launching a three-year project using UAS to monitor hurricanes and help scientists better understand why tropical storms become hurricanes, and what signs predict the metamorphosis. Scientists have been unable to determine why or how some storms strengthen so rapidly. UAS are able to fly straight through hurricane clouds to measure conditions, something manned flights and satellites cannot do.

    - Nicholls State protecting the Gulf Coast – Nicholls State University is using a six-foot UAS to map the Louisiana coast. Louisiana's barrier islands are an important habitat for migratory birds, as well as the first line of defence against hurricanes. Erosion of the island has damaged the habitat, as well as the important protective function the islands serve. By flying more frequently and hover longer than satellites or manned aircraft, the UAS save money and provide a better picture of the situation on the coast.

- **Mitigating Disasters**
    - Helping rescue efforts following Hurricane Katrina – UAS were used to help search and rescue teams in the aftermath of Hurricane Katrina. Scientists from the University of South Florida worked with Florida rescuers in Mississippi, in what was the first known use of small UAS for an actual disaster. Brought in to survey Pearlington, MS, within two hours, the responders had the data from the UAVs showing that no survivors were trapped and that the flood waters from the cresting Pearl River were not posing an additional threat.

    - Surveying damage caused by flooding of the Red River – UAS aided the response to the severe flooding of the Red River in the upper Midwest in April 2011. According to the U.S. Customs and Border Protections Office, which leant the UAS to the effort, the UAS mapped more than 800 nautical miles along the flooded tributaries and basins in Minnesota and North Dakota, and provided streaming video and analysis of the areas affected by the flood such as levee integrity and ice damming. The information provided by UAS gave forecasters more accurate predictions of when and where the flooding would be at its worst.

- o Assessing fallout from the damaged Fukushima nuclear plant – After Japan was struck by a devastating, earthquake-induced tsunami on March 11, 2011, a nuclear facility in Fukushima began to leak dangerous levels of radiation, making it impossible for emergency responders to approach the facility's reactors. A UAS from America was used to fly over the damaged facility and use advanced sensors to help responders gain situational awareness they were prevented from otherwise obtaining due to the radiation.

Potential Future Uses

- **Enhancing Public Safety**
    - o Enhancing search and rescue efforts – In January 2012, the Mesa (CO) County Sheriff's office purchased small UAS to assist in search and rescue operations. The UAS can cover wide swaths of land and uses cameras and infrared imaging to send video to ground controllers. The use of UAS is also cheap, with the direct operational cost totaling $3.36 per hour. In addition to aiding search and rescue missions, it could also help fight wildfires by determining hotspots and improving situational awareness.

- **Enabling Scientific Research**
    - o Safely tracking fish and wildlife – After colleagues were killed in a helicopter crash, Idaho fish biologist Phil Groves has led an effort to develop small, maneuverable UAS for use tracking fish and wildlife. Currently in a multi-year test, Groves says the use of UAS could be a safer and more affordable way to count fish nests than the traditional way of using helicopters.

- **Mitigating Disasters**
    - o Enabling communications following a disaster – The Federal Communications Commission is examining the use of UAS to help with communication relays in the event of a disaster to ensure emergency responders are able to communicate with each other. Following Hurricane Katrina, dozens of 911 call centers were knocked out of commission. UAS could help ensure connectivity until land-based communications are restored.

    - o Assisting in oil spill response – The University of Alaska Fairbanks is testing UAS focused on improving oil spill response and clean up capabilities in difficult terrain and conditions. The technology gathers 3-D aerial data to produce a detailed image of the affected area, and allows oil spill responders to complete shoreline clean-up and assessment survey work with minimal impact on the shoreline or critical habitat.

- **Supporting Agriculture**
    - o Helping farmers fight disease in crops – Researchers at the University of Florida are developing helicopter-style UAS to help farmers detect diseases and stress in their crops. Using GPS technology, the UAS take photographs and measurements and are proving particularly useful for citrus growers, allowing producers to easily detect tree health problems that aren't visible to the human eye.

- **Expanding Commercial Uses**
    - o Monitoring energy infrastructure – Energy companies have been testing small UAS to potentially be used to monitor miles of pipeline and drilling rigs. Rather than using manned helicopters that cost an average of $300 per hour to operate, UAS could provide a more cost-effective alternative. UAS ability to go into areas too hazardous for humans also holds potential for energy companies. The flames produced by crude processing operations can jump as high as 300 feet in seconds, making it too dangerous for manned aircraft to survey maintenance needs without shutting down the operation. Using small UAS, however, allows companies to take pictures of the equipment while the flares are burning.

AUVSI
ASSOCIATION FOR UNMANNED
VEHICLE SYSTEMS INTERNATIONAL

Unmanned Aircraft Systems:
Current and Future Uses

Past/Current Uses

- **Enhancing Public Safety**
    o Fighting wildfires in California – In 2008, NASA assisted the state of California in fighting wildfires with the use of Ikhana, a UAS equipped with advanced technology. The information about the fires collected by Ilkhana was transmitted to command centers within minutes, and then distributed into the field giving firefighters crucial situational awareness. Throughout the operation, NASA pilots operating Ilkhana were in close communication with the FAA to ensure its safe separation from other aircraft.

    o Finding missing persons in New Mexico – On January 9, 2012, an Oklahoma couple became lost in the White Sands National Monument in New Mexico. UAS were brought in to assist with the search. Once the couple's location was pinpointed, the UAS relayed specific coordinates of the couple and monitored their location and movement as rescue helicopters were en route.

    o Patrolling the U.S.-Mexico border – The U.S. Customs and Border Patrol use unmanned systems to patrol the U.S.-Mexico border, helping prevent drug smuggling and potential terrorist threats. The UAS monitor areas, which would take agents on the ground days to reach.

- **Enabling Scientific Research**
    o NASA studying hurricanes – NASA is launching a three-year project using UAS to monitor hurricanes and help scientists better understand why tropical storms become hurricanes, and what signs predict the metamorphosis. Scientists have been unable to determine why or how some storms strengthen so rapidly. UAS are able to fly straight through hurricane clouds to measure conditions, something manned flights and satellites cannot do.

    o Nicholls State protecting the Gulf Coast – Nicholls State University is using a six-foot UAS to map the Louisiana coast. Louisiana's barrier islands are an important habitat for migratory birds, as well as the first line of defence against hurricanes. Erosion of the island has damaged the habitat, as well as the important protective function the islands serve. By flying more frequently and hover longer than satellites or manned aircraft, the UAS save money and provide a better picture of the situation on the coast.

- **Mitigating Disasters**
    o Helping rescue efforts following Hurricane Katrina – UAS were used to help search and rescue teams in the aftermath of Hurricane Katrina. Scientists from the University of South Florida worked with Florida rescuers in Mississippi, in what was the first known use of small UAS for an actual disaster. Brought in to survey Pearlington, MS, within two hours, the responders had the data from the UAVs showing that no survivors were trapped and that the flood waters from the cresting Pearl River were not posing an additional threat.

    o Surveying damage caused by flooding of the Red River – UAS aided the response to the severe flooding of the Red River in the upper Midwest in April 2011. According to the U.S. Customs and Border Protections Office, which leant the UAS to the effort, the UAS mapped more than 800 nautical miles along the flooded tributaries and basins in Minnesota and North Dakota, and provided streaming video and analysis of the areas affected by the flood such as levee integrity and ice damming. The information provided by UAS gave forecasters more accurate predictions of when and where the flooding would be at its worst.

- Assessing fallout from the damaged Fukushima nuclear plant – After Japan was struck by a devastating, earthquake-induced tsunami on March 11, 2011, a nuclear facility in Fukushima began to leak dangerous levels of radiation, making it impossible for emergency responders to approach the facility's reactors. A UAS from America was used to fly over the damaged facility and use advanced sensors to help responders gain situational awareness they were prevented from otherwise obtaining due to the radiation.

Potential Future Uses

- **Enhancing Public Safety**
    - Enhancing search and rescue efforts – In January 2012, the Mesa (CO) County Sheriff's office purchased small UAS to assist in search and rescue operations. The UAS can cover wide swaths of land and uses cameras and infrared imaging to send video to ground controllers. The use of UAS is also cheap, with the direct operational cost totaling $3.36 per hour. In addition to aiding search and rescue missions, it could also help fight wildfires by determining hotspots and improving situational awareness.

- **Enabling Scientific Research**
    - Safely tracking fish and wildlife – After colleagues were killed in a helicopter crash, Idaho fish biologist Phil Groves has led an effort to develop small, maneuverable UAS for use tracking fish and wildlife. Currently in a multi-year test, Groves says the use of UAS could be a safer and more affordable way to count fish nests than the traditional way of using helicopters.

- **Mitigating Disasters**
    - Enabling communications following a disaster – The Federal Communications Commission is examining the use of UAS to help with communication relays in the event of a disaster to ensure emergency responders are able to communicate with each other. Following Hurricane Katrina, dozens of 911 call centers were knocked out of commission. UAS could help ensure connectivity until land-based communications are restored.

    - Assisting in oil spill response – The University of Alaska Fairbanks is testing UAS focused on improving oil spill response and clean up capabilities in difficult terrain and conditions. The technology gathers 3-D aerial data to produce a detailed image of the affected area, and allows oil spill responders to complete shoreline clean-up and assessment survey work with minimal impact on the shoreline or critical habitat.

- **Supporting Agriculture**
    - Helping farmers fight disease in crops – Researchers at the University of Florida are developing helicopter-style UAS to help farmers detect diseases and stress in their crops. Using GPS technology, the UAS take photographs and measurements and are proving particularly useful for citrus growers, allowing producers to easily detect tree health problems that aren't visible to the human eye.

- **Expanding Commercial Uses**
    - Monitoring energy infrastructure – Energy companies have been testing small UAS to potentially be used to monitor miles of pipeline and drilling rigs. Rather than using manned helicopters that cost an average of $300 per hour to operate, UAS could provide a more cost-effective alternative. UAS ability to go into areas too hazardous for humans also holds potential for energy companies. The flames produced by crude processing operations can jump as high as 300 feet in seconds, making it too dangerous for manned aircraft to survey maintenance needs without shutting down the operation. Using small UAS, however, allows companies to take pictures of the equipment while the flares are burning

Æ

Made in the USA
Las Vegas, NV
18 November 2024